CHIPPENDALE

BENEATH THE FACTORY WALL

CHIPPENDALE

BENEATH THE FACTORY WALL

SHIRLEY FITZGERALD

HALSTEAD PRESS

SYDNEY MMVIII

This edition published by Halstead Press
Unit 66, 89 Jones Street
Ultimo, New South Wales, 2007

and

Gorman House
Ainslie Avenue
Braddon, Australian Capital Territory, 2612

In association with the City of Sydney

First edition 1990, Hale and Iremonger Pty Limited

National Library cataloguing in publication entry

Fitzgerald, Shirley, 1949-
    Chippendale: beneath the factory wall.

    Includes index.
    ISBN 9781920831486

    1. Chippendale (N.S.W.) – History. I. Title.
    (Series: Sydney history series).

Chippendale: Beneath the Factory Wall is a publication of the City of Sydney's History Program

CONTENTS

ACKNOWLEDGEMENTS

This book is part of the Sydney City Council's History Project. The idea of writing a history to commemorate the Sesquicentenary of its incorporation in 1842 arose from discussions between the Manager of Records and Archives Services, Janet Howse, and the Town Clerk, Leon Carter, and was accepted by the Council in 1986. Several smaller studies of various geographic areas of the city have also been undertaken, including this one on Chippendale.

The Council's foresight in funding this project and the generosity in sharing knowledge and skills which has been extended to me by Council's officers have greatly assisted in the preparation of this book. The advisory committee established by the Council to oversee the project, chaired by Graham Joss, the deputy Town Clerk, and containing historians from the outside community, as well as Council officers, has always been supportive. So too have the staff of the Records and Archives Services Branch of the Information Systems Department under the direction of Kerry Nash. The manuscript was read by Janet Howse, Council's Archives Officers Sigrid McCausland and Anne Picot, and Heather Radi, who is a member of the advisory committee; all were generous and constructive in their comments. While they are not responsible for the text, it is better for their suggestions.

Many other people within Council were helpful, but special mention must be made of Larry Cahill, the plans custodian in the City Engineers' Department, and Dennis Robbie and Amanda Frick of the same department, who drew several new maps of Chippendale.

Christopher Keating, who has worked with me as research assistant on this project, has been both diligent and creative in his approach to locating material for the book, and has contributed considerably to its final form through conversation, ideas and criticism.

One of the most satisfying aspects of writing this book has come from talking to residents and ex-residents of Chippendale. Walking through Chippendale's streets in the company of people who know them intimately and listening to accounts of experiences and reminiscences helped to increase my understanding. I also learned how much people want their history to be written, and I hope they will derive some satisfaction and interest from this book. Thanks are due to many people, but especially to John Chippendale, Ray Cowling, Sonny Glynn, Edith Hughes, Mavis Kenny, Barry Little, Lois McEvoy, Laura McRae, Ted O'Connell (Tooths and Company), Ken Prentice, E.A. Shepherd, Ron Sutton and Margaret Watts. I first met Margaret at the Council's archives when she was researching details of her Chippendale house and, for no other reason than that she 'wanted to know', she contributed many hours of voluntary research to this project.

Many people provided material and information in their professional capacity: Sarah Walters, the City Librarian; and the staff of the City Library, the State Library of New South Wales, the Mitchell Library, and the State Archives Office; Maureen Purtell at the Archives of Business and Labour (Australian National University); the Colonial Sugar Refinery's Sydney office (then located in O'Connell Street); Ross Duker of the Australian Bureau of Statistics; Pat Hodgkinson, the archivist for Grace Brothers Department store; and Bob

Leonard of Westpac Museum. Jan Burnswoods and Jim Fletcher of NSW Department of Education History Unit provided information on schools, and the Sydney City Mission gave permission for me to consult its records held in the Mitchell Library.

Many of these institutions provided photographs and maps, as did the Council, several other organisations and individuals. These are all acknowledged in the list of photographic sources at the end of the book. John Prescott produced excellent copies of old images which were often of dubious quality, Adrian Hall took care to represent present-day Chippendale in the best possible light and Robert Cameron allowed the copy of Freak's portrait of his ancestor Robert Cooper to be photographed. Alan Walker and Sylvia Griffin compiled the index. Heather Cam at Hale and Iremonger edited the manuscript with skill and patience.

While all this assistance is acknowledged, final responsibility for the content of the book lies with me. I have appreciated above all else the professional way in which the Council of the City of Sydney has allowed the work to be written without editorial restraint, so that what was written might be a history and not an apology.

2008

It is many years since this book was first written. It was the first of a number of precinct studies that also included histories of Surry Hills, Millers Point and Pyrmont and Ultimo. The City's decision to update and reissue these out-of-print books was made in the belief that they continue to fill a useful role, and because these inner city areas currently hold very different populations, and therefore, a new generation of readers.

The text has been lightly edited to correct minor inaccuracies and a postscript added. Needless to say, I would approach the writing of a history of Chippendale differently if I were writing it now. But the dominant theme, of the uneven contest for scarce resources of urban space, land and amenities, remains important.

For this edition the City's archives staff updated the references to conform to current practice and planner Cathy Cusack provided guidance on the inclusion of new material. At Halstead Press Matthew Richardson and Alana Ayliffe oversaw the editing and production and Judi Rowe developed the new design. As ever, any shortcomings or misrepresentations in the text are mine.

Shirley Fitzgerald

ABBREVIATIONS

ABS	Australian Bureau of Statistics		Australian National University
ADB	*Australian Dictionary of*	NSCA	City of Sydney Archives
	Biography	NSW	New South Wales
CCS	Council of City of Sydney	*NSWPD*	*New South Wales Parliamentary*
CHO	City Health Officer		*Debates*
CRS	Council Record Series	*NSW V&P*	*New South Wales Votes and*
CSR	Colonial Sugar Refinery		*Proceedings*
GP	Government Printer	*PC*	*Proceedings of Council* (Council of
JRAHS	*Journal of the Royal Australian*		the City of Sydney)
	Historical Society	RC	Resolution of Council
LA	Legislative Assembly	SC	Select Committee
LC	Legislative Council	*SCSSHB*	*Sydney City and Suburban Sewage*
LMM	Lord Mayoral Minute		*and Health Board*
LTO	Land Titles Office	*SMH*	*Sydney Morning Herald*
MAAS	Power House Museum	SRNSW	State Records of New South
ML SLNSW	Mitchell Library, State Library		Wales
	of New South Wales	TCR	Town Clerk's Report
NBAC	Noel Butlin Archives Centre,		

CONVERSIONS

Distance, length

1 mile	=	1.61 km
1 kilometre	=	0.62 mile
1 foot (ft)	=	30.5 cm
1 metre (m)	=	3.28 ft

Area

100 acres (ac)	=	40.5 hectares (ha)

Water Volume

10 gallons	=	45.5 litres (1)

Weight

100 ounces (oz)	=	2.83 kg
100 pounds (lb)	=	45.36 kg
1 ton	=	1.02 tonne

INTRODUCTION

THIS BOOK tells the story of the development of Chippendale, a small and unpretentious area of the city, behind Broadway, wedged between Central Railway and Sydney University.

Today it is densely covered in housing, most of it of late nineteenth century vintage, and small scale industrial buildings, most of them dating from the early twentieth century. The main exception to this is the decommissioned Carlton Brewery (previously Tooths) which covers a large portion of Chippendale with concrete paving and an assortment of new and old buildings. Only the surprisingly healthy gardens emerging in the renovated terraces of Chippendale's latest home buyers and the street landscaping of the City Council give a clue to the fertile soil beneath. Chippendale, before European settlement and degradation of the area began, was covered in generous vegetation and rich soil, traversed by several creeks which ultimately found their way into Blackwattle Swamp.

Its original inhabitants would have viewed this natural abundance with an eye to conserving its food-supplying qualities, but white settlers saw in these same conditions, and especially in the availability of fresh water, potential for industrial development.

The history of European settlement here has always been tied up with industry, and at no time has Chippendale been a 'desired' address. Indeed, with time, it became less frequently an address for residents at all, as factories encroached upon its streets of nineteenth-century housing. Only in recent decades has this process begun to be reversed.

Explanations for the area becoming industrial have in part to do with the way private property owners saw their maximum advantage through this use of their land. But in part the process was accelerated by deliberate decisions of the colonial government and the City Council that were based on the assumption that this was the proper way for development to go in Chippendale. In particular, the emergence of the town planning movement, which had close links with the Council, encouraged the rapid transition of residential places considered to be slums, to industrial and commercial uses, in the early twentieth century.

Parts of Chippendale, along with other inner city areas, were publically resumed for private industrial benefit, thereby contributing to the area's social decline.

This book recounts some of the skirmishes in the battle for territorial control of Chippendale. The first two chapters deal with the first phase of development, when the industrial buildings of the early colonial manufacturers who amassed wealth in Chippendale dominated the scene. In contrast, the housing of the people who worked for these industrialists was mean and insubstantial and their local environment became ever more degraded. The nexus between the wealth of the few and the poverty of most of Chippendale's inhabitants, so ill rewarded for their labours, was plain to see.

Chapter Three, which deals with the period from 1880 until World War I, covers a complex time when some of Chippendale's industrial land, previously controlled by the Colonial Sugar Company, was subdivided for residential use. However the greed of the

'The road to Parramatta, from the Sydney Tollbar as far as Cooper's Distillery, is a disgrace to the Government, and an imposition on the public' (*Sydney Gazette*, 28 January 1834).

developers, which had prompted them to subdivide illegally, came up against the new found town-planning interests of the City Council, and a battle ensued over the question of what were appropriate standards for urban residential subdivision. By the time the question was resolved, the most residential phase of Chippendale's development was on the wane, and much of this land was again used by industry.

In the competition between residential and industrial users of Chippendale's land, the Council played an ambivalent role. In the provision of amenities, such as sewage and water, it responded to conflicting demands of wealthy ratepayers—in this case industrialists—and numerous, but less powerful, residents. In the final chapter we encounter the Council playing the role of deliberate promoter of Chippendale as an industrial area, resuming land specifically to promote industrial/commercial development. However, competing forces within the Council resulted in the construction of the Strickland Buildings, the Council's first foray into public housing. These were some of Sydney's earliest flats.

The book is also about the lives of the people who lived and worked in Chippendale. They were, for the most part, some of Sydney's poorest citizens. The forces which made some individuals rich also required the maintenance of a poorly paid and insecure workforce in the same area. Later, with more worker mobility, the prior evolution of the area into one of depressed housing and few amenities ensured that it would remain poor.

Reports of government investigators in the nineteenth and early twentieth centuries frequently highlighted the dirt and disease of the area. This was usually linked to value judgements about the inhabitants, who were often portrayed as anything from unstable to immoral. Only very rarely do we hear the voices and opinions of the people of Chippendale themselves until the present, when we can go and 'collect' remembrances of people who have lived there. Rarely will these stretch back as far as the beginning of the twentieth century, and before that we have only our imaginations to rely on. These we must employ if we are to begin to achieve any clear understanding of the place as experienced by its inhabitants, as well as by outside observers.

In the early twentieth century, social workers and middle class reformers often predicted the death of such inner city residential areas and exulted in the new era dawning where everyone would live happily and healthfully in suburbia. On the other hand, residents of Chippendale and other similar city areas often remember life in these parts with affection and pride. They talk of a sense of community, of neighbourliness and caring which their less fortunate suburban counterparts missed out on. They recall skills and survival techniques which outside observers denigrated or missed seeing completely.

None of these rememberings negates the truth of the hardships endured or the drudgery undergone, but they recall much that is rich beyond the reach of conventional wealth. The historian, bequeathed a substantial amount of critical material generated mostly by outsiders looking in on Chippendale, must tread carefully, if the lives of the women and men who have lived there are not to be submerged in the judgements of those who thought they knew better and considered Chippendale an unfit place to live. Some of the grimmer realities of life in Chippendale were generated by the behaviour of the very people who rejected such areas. All areas of the city and the metropolis are parts of the whole, with the wealth of some areas being supported by the poverty of others. Notions of wealth and poverty are complex, and there has been much of both in Chippendale.

Balfour Street, Chippendale, c.1910.

1

EARLY CHIPPENDALE TO 1850

O<small>N THE EVENING</small> of November 1817 James Harris and an unknown companion decided to augment their meagre diets, or line their pockets, or both, by stealing potatoes from one of the farms a bit further down the road from the government brickyards where they had toiled all day under the hot summer sun. The evening was moonlit, which helped them to negotiate their way across the land belonging to William Chippendale, some of which was boggy in the vicinity of the Blackwattle Swamp Stream. Unfortunately for the two convicts, the light also allowed Chippendale to see them. He had left his house just after ten o'clock to round up some straying cattle, and on his way back home noticed the figures in his potato field. He shouted at them to stop, or he would shoot. The men, carrying a sack of potatoes, began to run. Chippendale fired his double-barrelled gun and James Harris was shot dead.

Chippendale made a voluntary confession of his crime, in which he noted that he had been frequently robbed of produce and fowls, and that on the previous night four hundredweight of potatoes had gone missing. The fact that he was carrying a loaded gun suggests that he was constantly prepared for the possibility of pillage, but he seemed to regret that events had turned out so badly. John Kent, a labourer from a neighbouring farm whom Chippendale had called to his assistance, told the coroner that 'he told me he had killed a man for which he appeared very sorry,' while another witness, who had walked Chippendale back to his house, claimed that 'he had expressed that he himself was an unfortunate man and that a cloud seemed to hang over him.'[1] Chippendale was possibly referring to the fact that Henrietta, his wife, had died earlier in the year, leaving a large and youthful family. But however black the skies seemed to William Chippendale, his most recent misfortune seems not to have had any serious long term repercussions. His immediate and contrite confession would have gone in his favour, and besides, the times were not kind to the likes of convict James Harris.[2]

These details, gleaned from the coroner's inquest into the death of James Harris, give us an early glimpse of the area of Sydney which bears the name of Chippendale. It is a small area that has long been perceived as part of the old 'centre' of Sydney, but clearly there was a time when Chippendale was rural.

The focus of white settlement in Sydney began at the docks on Port Jackson, and even as late as the 1830s or 1840s most people would have thought of the town as terminating in the vicinity of Bathurst and Liverpool streets. Beyond this were the steep slopes of

---

1 Evidence at inquest into death of James Harris, 19 November 1817, SRNSW: NRS [2/8286 pp 197–206].
2 *Sydney Gazette*, 20 December 1817.

Brickfield Hill. Here, from the early years, convicts toiled at making bricks and felling trees for the growing settlement.

The slopes were dotted with claypits and charcoal kilns, and the road into town was well trodden by gangs of yoked convicts cursing and sweating as they pulled cartloads of wares. In 1819 barracks were built nearby (on the present day Central Railway, Belmore Park area) to house 200 male convict workers, while another barracks building, separated by a high wall, housed an additional 100 youths. In 1821 part of this complex of buildings became the Benevolent Asylum—Sydney's Poor House. The barracks sometimes doubled as a debtors' prison, and were used to house the dreaded treadmill from 1823 until 1846, when the establishment was closed and the instrument of torture transferred to Darlinghurst Goal. Men climbed endlessly, on hourly shifts, grinding up to half a ton of grain a day. [3]

These buildings were called Carters Barracks, because, as well as providing accommodation for the convicts who worked the brickfields, this was where government carts, horses, harnesses and so on were requisitioned. It is also said that convict carters bringing produce to market stayed at these barracks overnight. In deference to the steepness of the hill, and because of increasing chaos around the George Street Markets further along the road into town, in 1829 Governor Darling established cattle markets near the Barracks. Later, in 1834, hay markets were also held in the area. [4] Related to this, a number of taverns became established to quench the thirst before the long haul up into town, to accommodate the traveller in town on the evening before market day, or to provide a last drink at town prices for brave souls heading the other way, beyond the confines of settlement. From 1838, the hill was not so steep after convicts were set to work

This sketch, c.1820, shows Chippendale as bushland beyond the end of town. The cottage, barely visable on the right, is Ultimo House.

3 Frank Clune, *Saga of Sydney* (1961) pp 201–03.
4 Michael Christie, *The Sydney Markets, 1788–1988* (1988) p 51; 'Old Chum' (J. M. Forde) in 'Old Sydney', *Truth*, 7 July 1912. (This long running column in *Truth* will be referred to as 'Old Chum', with the date. A consolidated scrapbook collection of these articles is held by the ML.)

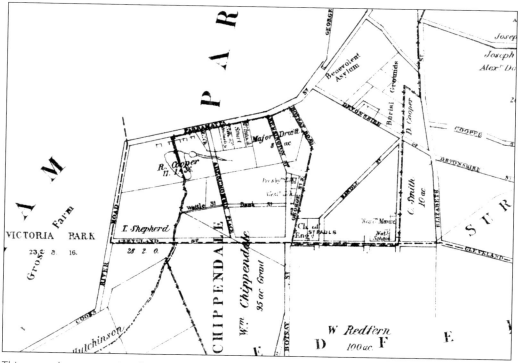

This map, drawn sometime later in the 19th century, clearly shows the grants to Chippendale, and Cooper's Dam.

'cutting and paring off the higher part of the road' and 'upwards of one million cubic feet of rubble changed its situation by manual labour'.[5] Henceforth those who trod the road would have less of a haul.

This then was the edge of Sydney, where urban structures did not yet dominate scenes of government men toiling, and where cattle and horses were stabled for market or roamed in the Government paddocks. At the intersection of George and Pitt streets, Macquarie had a toll gate erected in 1811 to raise revenue for the upkeep of the road to Parramatta. Here the road changed its name from George Street to Parramatta Street, and just east of Parramatta Street, almost parallel with it, ran a stream of fresh water which eventually crossed the road under a bridge and drained into Blackwattle Swamp. Beyond this stream, Chippendale held his grant of land.[6]

The original grant, opposite the Ultimo Estate, adjoined the farms of Redfern, Chisholm and Hutchinson. On the south side it terminated at the Blackwattle Swamp Stream, one of several which drained this low-lying area. In part the land was boggy, in part rich soil, suitable for intensive agriculture. Nearby on the town side were the military gardens, and next door to the west lived Thomas Rushton, Henrietta Chippendale's father. Later Shepherd's Nursery, for many years a landmark in the neighbourhood, would be

---

5 Maclehose, 1888, quoted in Frank Clune, *Saga of Sydney*, pp 145–46.
6 Copy of Chippendale's grant at LTO Deed, packet 1236, Document 2.

established here joining Chippendale's grant. By mid-century, when factories and houses began to dominate this 95-acre estate, old timers were fond of harking back to the early days when waterfowl and watercress flourished in the creeks.

This is how it would have been in 1815 for William Chippendale and his wife Henrietta, née Rushton, newly arrived from Liverpool, Lancashire. The Chippendales arrived as free settlers: William bearing a formal letter of introduction from Lord Bathurst of the Colonial Office; Henrietta in charge of a large family, the youngest a baby, born at sea and named Hebe, after the ship that had carried them all to New South Wales.[7] The Colonial Office at this time neither encouraged nor discouraged free settlers, but Bathurst did require of them that they be able to pay their own passage and have £500 capital. This was not always achieved, according to Governor Macquarie, who looked with little favour on immigrants who came expecting government support. To those with capital and enterprise, he granted land, sold livestock, and hired out convict labour, on similar terms as applied to emancipists.[8] Because Chippendale came officially recommended and already had relations in the colony, and because Macquarie granted him land so close to Sydney, where most land had already been alienated, we may suppose that the family was tolerably secure financially.

The ninety-five acres were granted on condition that Chippendale cleared and cultivated at least twenty acres within five years, during which time he could not sell any of the land. This grant is dated 1819, but in all probability the land was made available as soon as the Chippendales arrived in Sydney. Occupation before the formalities of the grant were completed was common in the early decades of the colony, and Macquarie specifically permitted it, in recognition that the official surveys could not keep pace with the genuine demand for land. After 1816, and until the end of his governorship, there was a rapid rise in population and a high demand for food, with the percentage of inhabitants on the government store actually increasing in 1816, and 1817. In such circumstances Macquarie placed the encouragement of land cultivation above clarity of land tenure.[9]

By 1817, at least, the Chippendales were well established on the banks of the Blackwattle Swamp Creek. They had built a house and quarters for 'a government man', were running cattle, growing potatoes and had planted a field of barley.[10] Whether this farming venture was a success or not is unclear. By 1820 Chippendale had purchased a public house and land in Sydney town, and continued for a number of years as a publican, but he also subsequently held land in other parts of the colony.[11] In 1821 he sold his Chippendale Estate to Solomon Levey for £380, well before his five years of compulsory tenure was up, if counted from 1819, the year of the grant, but probably five years in fact since he had taken possession of it.

7 Colonial Office Despatches, 202/8 Bathurst to Macquarie, 6 December 1814; death certificate, John Giles Chippendale, 30 June 1886.
8 Brian Fletcher, *Landed Enterprise and Penal Society* (1976) pp 17, 129–30.
9 Ibid, pp 122–24.
10 SRNSW: NRS 5602 [2/8286].
11 LTO Book 8, No 258, 259.

Solomon Levey, convict turned colonial business tycoon, invested his profits from trading, shipping, whaling and banking in real estate. He eventually owned most of Alexandria, Redfern and Waterloo, as well as vast amounts of land in the eastern suburbs and rural New South Wales. During the 1820s he sold off parcels of Chippendale land, much of it to William Hutchinson, convict turned public servant and large landholder. But much of it was untouched, and when Levey died in London in 1833, his colonial land holdings included 32½ acres of unsubdivided land in Chippendale.[12]

However, by the time this land came on the market in 1838, substantial developments had occurred elsewhere in Chippendale, particularly in the area adjoining the Chippendale grant, between the creek and Parramatta Street. These were, most notably, Cooper's Brisbane Distillery and Tooth's Kent Brewery, both industries which became synonymous with the name of Chippendale.

Of these two establishments, the distillery came first, disappeared early, and enjoyed a turbulent history in between. It was built in 1825 on a land grant of just over seventeen acres made by Governor Brisbane to Robert Cooper in June of that year. Cooper, convicted for receiving stolen goods to the value of £3000 in 1812, was transported to Sydney for four years in 1813, but pardoned in 1818. Possibly using finance brought with him from England, he set up a store in George Street and quickly became established in Sydney's business circles.[13] He had owned a couple of public houses in London and had operated various shady affairs prior to his forcible removal to New South Wales. In his new country he continued in much the same vein. He quickly gained fame for his tempestuous lifestyle and his addiction to speculative and illegal manipulations of men and institutions. His business activities were frequently not much this side of bankruptcy, and several times he used the Insolvency Courts to avoid paying unwelcome debts.

Bob Cooper, also known as Robert the Large, is variously described by a descendant as

> *'a cheerful intelligent man with twinkling black eyes', by a recent historian as 'a stout, kindhearted man', by a contemporary colonist as a 'bloated lump of flesh and very vulgar'.[14] Whatever interpretation is put on the man, he was without doubt a 'colourful character'. His frequent court appearances both as plaintiff and defendant, have left a legacy of descriptions of this man, such as that of W. C. Wentworth, who wrote to Cooper's solicitor on behalf of a beleaguered client, regretting that 'Mr Robert Cooper who is so liberal of his Gin to others, should not have indulged Mr Alexander with a taste of it last night, instead of that taste which he gave him of a bludgeon'.[15]*

---

12 LTO Deed packet 1236, Documents 2 and 4.

13 R.L. Knight, 'Cooper, Robert (1776–1857)' *Australian Dictionary of Biography*, Vol. 1, 1966, p 246; CSR (Syd) A5.0.8, Document 7, title deed as transferred to Robey, Irving and Knox, 1853. CSR records were consulted in the company's head office in Sydney—cited as CSR (Syd) and at the Archives of Business and Labour, ANU, Canberra (cited as ANU).

14 F.M. Edmonds, 'Cooper, Robert, NSW, 1813' in *Pioneer Women*, pp 85–87; R.L.Knight, op. cit.; 'Old Chum', 12 June 1910; *SMH*, 27 May 1843.

15 Wentworth Papers, ML MS, A1 440, p 237.

Cooper's association with gin production predated 1825 and his Chippendale grant, with an earlier distillery being built on Old South Head Road soon after distilling was legalised in 1822. Here too, in 1824, the family residence, Juniper Hall, had been built. The name, referring to the juniper berry which is an essential ingredient of gin, was no doubt chosen in defiance of more refined colonial traditions in house naming. But the location, east of the city, placed Cooper with the colony's wealthy. In this his behaviour was typical of Chippendale's capitalists. Not then nor since have they chosen to live in Chippendale.

One early settler of wealth who did live nearby was Dr John Harris, of the Ultimo Estate, on Parramatta Street opposite the site of Robert Cooper's new Brisbane Distillery built in the second half of 1825. Cooper apparently made free with timber from Harris's land in the building of it, for in September Harris was instructing Wentworth, his solicitor, to instigate an action against Cooper for illegally 'cutting and slashing' on the estate. Cooper's reaction to this was to offer an out of court settlement (which Harris declined) and at the same time to offer him £4000 for the purchase of Ultimo (which Harris also declined).[16] The offer was a bold one, considering that an inquiry into the affairs of the Bank of New South Wales the following year indicated that Cooper, a principal shareholder, had direct and indirect liabilities to the bank in excess of twelve thousand pounds with 'little or no security'. Some of this loan would have been used to finance the distillery, which cost in excess of twenty thousand pounds.[17]

The Brisbane Distillery became an early colonial landmark. An 1829 description to accompany a panorama exhibited in Leicester Square, London, records:

> *an excellent range of buildings, entirely of freestone, situated on a stream of fresh water, with a mill, numerous store houses, and every convenience for carrying on an extensive business.*[18]

The estate of John Harris, across Parramatta Street from Chippendale. It was here that Cooper helped himself to timber for his building operations.

16 Ibid, pp 174, 194.
17 Report, Board of Inquiry, Bank of New South Wales, 12 May 1826, quoted in G. J. R. Linge, *Industrial Awakening* (1979), p 85.
18 Robert Burford, *Description of A View of the Town of Sydney* (1829), p 7.

Cooper's buildings were taken over by the Australasian Sugar Company in 1850. This 1860s painting of the Sugar Works would have shown essentially of the same buildings with some modifications and extentions. The buildings are shown from the rear, with the dam at capacity. On the horizon is the new university.

The people of Chippendale would have been amazed to think that people in London paid sixpence a time to see these illustrations of colonial life. The stream referred to was the Blackwattle Swamp Creek. It was the abundance of water which made Chippendale attractive to early industrialists, and this creek, along with the dam which Cooper built on it behind the distillery, was to play an important and varied role in the subsequent development of the area. The map on page 9 illustrates the location and extent of Cooper's holdings, including the dam, which at one time extended back from the distillery south to what is now Myrtle Street and almost to Abercrombie Place in the east.

Recollections of Cooper's dam, up until about the mid-century, tell of a place which was much valued by the local inhabitants for its aesthetic and recreational qualities. One oldtimer in 1910 recalled a garden on its banks, 'where most beautiful fruit grew, that was kept by a man named Conroy who was employed at Cooper's flour mill'. Another recollection was of a more sporting nature:

> In the early 50s there was a long-continued drought, and the dam dried up. It had long been a good fishing-ground for eels, and after school and working hours boys and men would go there with their fishing-lines and bait, to fish for eels. When darkness set in lines would be set; after tea they would be examined. Some would have fish on, and these would be re-set, and again looked at in the early morning. I have seen as many as twenty lines set there . . . The largest eel caught there was by a man named James Pamment, who lived in a little rubble-stone gunyah that was built at the same time

that Mr Cooper built the dam. Pamment and his sons were always called Plummer. The eel caught weighed 28³/4 pounds. Pamment, or Plummer, cut it up into pieces cross-wise, carried the pieces round on a barrow, and sold them for sixpence each.[19]

During the 1820s Cooper expanded his factory, so that by 1830 *The Australian* described 'gigantic buildings', comprised of 'a distillery, malting-stores, a pair of 40 horsepower steam engines, flour mills and ovens etc. etc. etc.' To all of this Cooper was adding a brewery, next to the quarry where stone for his buildings had been excavated. *The Australian* hoped his beer would equal the quality of his 'super excellent' whiskey, his 'excellent' gin and his 'execrable' rum.[20]

None of which should necessarily be believed. *The Australian* used this article as a vehicle for berating those who did not support colonial manufactures over 'any foreign sumptuary'. And while some descriptions compared Cooper's gin to the London article, others were far less complimentary.

In the various descriptions of Cooper's Parramatta Street works a number of activities are mentioned. A variety of individuals leased or worked the different functions of mill, sugar house, stores and so on. This was not unusual for early colonial enterprises, for with a small local market entrepreneurs with flexible plant, able to fulfil a variety of short term demands, were more likely to succeed than not. However, the implications of this were uneven output and unstable requirements for labour. The raw materials of distilling, brewing and milling were all seasonal and unevenly supplied, and possibly the plant was only rarely in full production.

Cooper himself was more inclined to wheeling and dealing than to steady production, and from 1829 onwards the distillery was mortgaged to finance other business interests or held by other family members. In 1843, a difficult year of depression and upheaval in the colonial economy, he discharged a longstanding mortgage on the property to the Bank of New South Wales, and immediately used the security of the property to borrow from the Union Bank. Heavily in debt, he chose this time to expand into extensive house construction in Chippendale (of which more will be said later) and then went into voluntary bankruptcy to avoid paying the constructors. By the end of the year he had regained the mortgaged property, but transferred it to one of his many children, the

---

ROYAL PANTECHNICON,

PARRAMATTA-STREET.

Under the patronage of His Excellency Sir Charles and Lady Mary Fitz Roy, His Excellency Sir Maurice and Lady O'Connell, and most of the *élite* of Sydney.

HIS Excellency the Governor has appointed Friday (this day), the 1st January, when he will open the Pantechnicon.

His Excellency and Lady Mary will be present in the forenoon, and the doors will open at ten o'clock, A.M. precisely, and continue open.

During the day, various pleasing amusements will be provided, and for the entertainment of visitors, the band of the 99th regiment, (who, by the kind permission of Colonel Despard, will be present) will afford that pleasure they are so well able to do. In addition, the services of some of the first-rate musical and vocal talent of the colony are secured for the occasion. And at night, a grand display of fireworks, such as are not known and were never seen in this colony, will be exhibited. These fireworks, which will be very beautiful, have been purchased at a great expense, and cannot fail to afford ample amusement.

Attached to the Pantechnicon is a large dam of water of eight acres, where boats will be in readiness for those who may so please to amuse themselves. Refreshments are provided in abundance, both day and night, and all who visit the Pantechnicon on the opening day cannot fail to be gratified.

The tickets for admission will be, single, 3s, double, 5s.

This will include day and night.

Tickets to be had of Mr. Aldis, George-street, and at the Pantechnicon, Parramatta-street.

By order of the Committee,
C. F. HEMMINGTON,
10602   Manager.

---

19 'Old Chum', 12 June 1910; 26 June 1910.
20 *The Australian*, 24 September 1830.

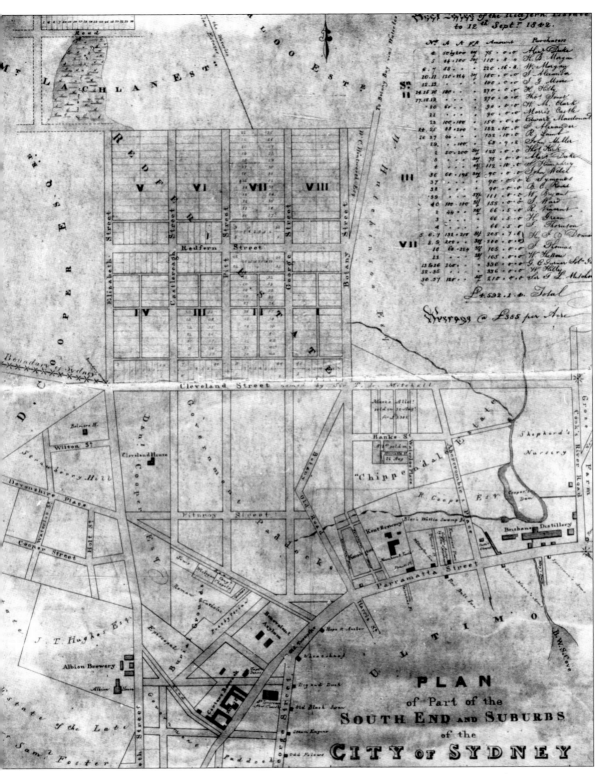

This map shows many of the places and features of Chippendale's development discussed in this chapter.

first son, also called Robert, for a promise of £35,000. In October of the following year it was back in Cooper the elder's hands, that is to say, they had torn up the promissory note, neither of them had exchanged any money, the bank still owned the property, and the local lawyers had added a little more lining to their pockets.[21] From about this time output was erratic, and advertisements appeared in the press announcing parts of the property for rent. For example, one of the stores, possibly the building erected in 1830 as a brewery, was sometimes recommended as a potential wool-washing plant.

One interesting venture was an attempt to use the larger of the two stores as a kind of bazaar or retail market place, managed by F. R. Hennington and called the Pantechnicon. The newspaper advertisements announcing the launching of this venture on New Year's Day 1847 claimed that Governor Fitzroy and Lady Fitzroy would attend and that the Band of the 99th Regiment would entertain the crowds, who were exhorted to buy, or promenade, or go for a row on the 'lake'. The venture, it was claimed, was under the patronage of 'most of the elite of Sydney', but it would seem that few of them, or indeed anyone else, attended the opening. A few days after New Year's Day, a newspaper announcement headed 'Royal Pantechnicon' explained that 'the races on Friday last having most materially affected our arrangements for that day, we were obliged to postpone the greater part of our amusements for another occasion.' People who had purchased tickets were advised to hold on to them until arrangements were made for a more suitable time.[22] It remains unclear how successful this early attempt at recycling industrial buildings for the purpose of entertainment was, but it was probably this enterprise James Scott recalled in 1910 when he described Cooper's Dam:

> When the dam was completed and full of water, Mr Cooper had a grand aquatic display, boats and tub racing and other ancient sports, including a greasy pole, a pig with a greased tail, etc. Some big official of the time was present to declare the dam open.[23]

It is possible that this recollection is correct, or it might be a remembrance of the Pantechnicon's opening in 1841. James

21 CSR (Syd), A5.0.8, Document 7.
22 SMH, 1 January 1847, 5 January 1847.
23 'Old Chum', 12 June 1910.

Scott, who would have been about eighteen or twenty at the time, worked for James Pemmell, who started out as a baker, but by 1850 was renting Cooper's steam flour mill next to the now disused Pantechnicon.

By 1849 Cooper faced mounting debts and attempted to clear them by advertising the whole of his manufacturing property in Chippendale for rental in March. The following month with mortgage repayments in default he was declared bankrupt and was before the Insolvency Court. He had accumulated about £34,000 in bad debts, while he was himself in debt to the tune of £23,000. Everyone owed him and he owed everyone. He owed legal firms, labourers' wages and individuals who had lent him money. He owed Margaret Potts, the governess, five months' wages of £16.13.4, he owed the doctor and even the baker.[24] On 1 February 1850 the estate passed into the hands of R.J. Want, a solicitor who made a practice of acting for merchants seeking equitable distribution of the assets of bankrupts.[25] The Chippendale properties were put up for sale, and the notice of the sale provides us with a detailed inventory of Cooper's Chippendale empire.

However, Cooper was never one to make good his debts if he could help it, and he managed to regain control of the property at this auction, bidding £9500.[26] It seems that by transferring assets and property to his son, Cooper had avoided exposing his real wealth. Most of his real assets were held by others or mortgaged, and his personal property was valued at less than £1000. Even the gin in the vats was not legally his and therefore difficult to recover, as it seemed that 'Mr. A.E.H. Cooper has been conducting his father's business . . . purchased the molasses . . . paid the wages of the men' and so on. However, as the official assignee pointed out to the Commissioner of Insolvent Estates, this was no great loss, the

Looking towards Sydney Town from the Kent Brewery in the 1840s. The land in the foreground is in front of the brewery, used for many years to graze the brewery animals.

---

24 Insolvency schedule, 23 April 1849 SRNSW: NRS 13654, File No. 1898, [2/8832].
25 Ricahard Want, 'Want, Randolph John (1811–1869)', *ADB*, Vol. 6, 1976, pp 349–50.
26 CSR (Syd), A5.0.8, Document 7.

Kent Brewery drays and horses, equipped for making short runs to local public houses.

spirits being 'of a very inferior description'. It seems that Cooper may even have deliberately blown up a vat at the distillery in order to avoid paying for it or to recover damages from the suppliers. John Struth, the manufacturing engineer who had supplied the machinery, and had not been paid, objected to Cooper's discharge from the Insolvency Court, not only because he believed Cooper had failed to make a full disclosure of his property, but because 'the said Insolvent hath in an action at law put a creditor to a vexatious or unjustifiable expense' by a 'frivolous' case.[27]

In 1852, Robert Cooper and several others who now shared an interest in the property, including Sarah, his third wife, and Daniel Cooper—another substantial but unrelated holder of Chippendale land—sold the whole lot to the Australasian Sugar Company, which paid £2,848.10.2 of 'lawful British money', and assumed the mortgage of £10,151.0.10. They acquired all the industrial and residential buildings mentioned in the newspaper advertisement reproduced on page 10. Much of the industrial property was run down and some of it not in use. The company paid off the mortgage in eighteen months and in 1854 began building a new refinery. Cooper's departure from Chippendale was followed not long afterwards by his death in May 1857, at the age of eighty.[28]

The second major industry in early Chippendale was Tooth's brewery, located on Parramatta Street, a little closer to town than the distillery. Its proprietors were as efficient and stable as Cooper was erratic and volatile, and the brewery experienced a well ordered and steady growth, employing ever-increasing numbers of workers and occupying ever-increasing amounts of land in Chippendale.

---

27 SRNSW: NRS 13654, File No. 1898, [2/8832].
28 *Pioneer Register*, Vol 1, 2nd edn.

In 1834 John Tooth purchased four and a half acres, originally part of a grant to Major Druitt, with the intention of building a brewery. He had considered acquiring brewing premises in the town, which at the time boasted about nine or ten small establishments, but rejected this in favour of a bolder plan. At this time the colony was booming, and substantial numbers of free settlers were arriving for the first time. Perhaps there was room for a larger brewery than the town had so far seen. The site, on the Blackwattle Swamp Creek, was a distance from the town, but there was plenty of room for expansion and ample fresh water in the streams which traversed this area, known as the Military Gardens.

John Tooth, a brewer and merchant, may have been the primary financial supporter of the venture, while his partner Charles Newnham was, according to one historian, 'the life and soul of the undertaking'.[29] By the end of 1834 the foundation stone was laid, and in October 1835 the Kent Brewery was formally opened, when 'drays were loaded with casks of the first brew and dispatched to the various customers who had sent in orders, after a vigorous canvass for orders by the Brewery travellers'. The complex, set well back from the road to allow space for drays and horses, consisted of an engine house, high chimney, offices, two storey stores, malt kilns and funnels, and cellars for storage of casks of ale and porter. There was also a private residence, Kent House, for John Tooth. The road from the Kent Brewery to this residence was called Kent Road.[30]

In 1843 the partnership of Newnham and Tooth was dissolved and John Tooth retired to his pastoral interests, but not before he had induced nephews Robert and Edwin Tooth, of Kent, England, to come to the colony and take over the business. They quickly decided that Chippendale was no new Kent, and chose to reside on the eastern side of the town of Sydney, but they, along with Frederick Tooth who joined them in 1853, had a long association with the brewery.[31]

As with Cooper's gin being manufactured next door, the product of the brewery received a varied press, but whatever its quality, it quickly acquired a large proportion of the market. However, that market was not extensive, partly because of a preference for imported beer amongst the upper crust of society, and partly because of a preference for spirits, especially rum and perhaps even Cooper's, among the lower orders. When a journalist was invited to tour the brewery in 1844, he was 'surprised at the extent and convenience' of it, but his description makes it clear that it was not in full production:

> The area of the malting floor . . . is 12,564 square feet, and the area within the whole of the entire building, 33,600 square feet. The two coppers contain about 3,500 gallons, and with the present fixtures about 400 barrels a week could be made; and if it should be necessary, with very little additional expense, that quantity could be much increased.[32]

---

29 H.W.H. Huntington, 'History of the Brewing Trade of Australia', extract at ANU/NBAC, Tooth's, Z223, Box 6, Document 2.
30 Ibid.
31 John Webster, *The Early Breweries of Australia* (Typescript, nd), ML Q991/W.
32 *SMH*, 23 July 1844.

A decade later the brewery was expanding, with extensive new plant imported, 'which, upon a moderate calculation, will brew as much beer in one day as the present does in a week, besides avoiding night labour'—an early example of night shift work.[33]

The real extent of this expansion is unclear because in part the new machinery was to furnish a larger building erected after the original brewery burnt down in 1853. This fire broke out on 16 January, on a Sunday afternoon, when the brewery was not working and the boilers not stoked. By the time they did get up some steam, extensive damage had already occurred, and although the Mayor, the Superintendent of Police, military, corporation workers and insurance company engines all turned up promptly, for lack of water nothing was done to stop the blaze for several hours. The brewery itself did not have town water laid on as it relied on natural supplies, and the nearest water pipe was a three-inch main in Charles Street, 325 feet from the fire. When it was connected, it gave 'a miserable supply'. Faithful employees and helpful citizens moved stocks of barley and maize to safety, while others, more concerned to help themselves, were down in the cellars drinking 'to excess of whatever they could find'. The fire continued well into the following day, when the malt kiln roof gave in, destroying a great deal of malt, and vaults beneath the kiln exploded.[34]

This degree of disruption would have reduced a less resilient enterprise to its knees, but in the case of the Kent Brewery, it was used as an opportunity to update and import improved plant. It would long remain dominant on the industrial landscape of Chippendale.

By mid-century in addition to the distillery and the brewery, there was a small steam flour mill in Abercrombie Street run by Hugh Taylor, while according to the city's 1845 assessment books, George Wagg had a small soap and candle factory on Parramatta Street. Phillip Whalan claimed to run a ginger beer factory, described by the assessor as a skillion

---

33 *Illustrated Sydney News*, 16 June 1855; 'Old Chum', 26 June 1920.
34 *SMH*, 17 and 18 January 1853.

attached to a wooden stable. Shepherd's Darling Nursery, behind the distillery, fronting Newtown Road, was undoubtedly one of the most pleasant places in Chippendale. Thomas Shepherd's grant, promised in 1827 and formalised in 1835, stipulated that 'he should establish a nursery and fruit garden thereon within two years'. The grant also attempted to forestall any problems with neighbour Cooper by precluding Shepherd from ever suing him in the event of the nursery being flooded by the dam after rain. But though the nursery was a pleasant spot, its impact on Chippendale was limited, as nurseryman Shepherd did not design gardens for Chippendale's poor, and the results of his handiwork were best seen in the gardens of the wealthy of the eastern sections of the town.[35]

While Shepherd used the fine alluvial soils of this well drained area, the creek had encouraged other industries across the road in Ultimo, most notably slaughterhouses and associated piggeries. Although they were not actually in Chippendale, the effects on residents could not be avoided. Philip Coleman Williams, who lived in the area in the 1850s, in later life recalled that it had been possible at high tide to row a boat under Parramatta Street to Cooper's Distillery. He remembered the upper reaches of the swamp, across the road in Ultimo, with its slaughterhouse built on piles out over the creek. The area, known locally as 'Aude Colone Valley', was strewn with offal, which sometimes was washed out into the harbour and sometimes not. Here Mary O'Shea, or 'Pig Mary' as she was called, could be seen picking her way through the mud in search of offal and offcuts to feed to her pigs. These would in their turn be slaughtered at the creek. Vermin, as well as Mary, survived on the pickings; and Billy Foset, the rat catcher, allegedly extracted the rodents from a retaining wall on Parramatta Street with his bare hands.[36]

The earliest housing in Chippendale was associated with its industries. Cooper built a stone cottage, Brisbane, on his property; Tooth lived briefly in Kent House on his; and Shepherd's Darling Nursery contained a large house on Cooks River Road. There were other substantial dwellings on Old Botany Road (Regent Street), but by and large Chippendale housing was cramped and mean, occupied by labourers and poor people unable to afford housing closer to town. One of the first areas occupied was that between the distillery and the brewery, in narrow little streets running back from Parramatta Street. The map reproduced on page 9 shows two streets here, called Thomas Street and Emigrant Place. Emigrant Place became known later as Dalton's Place, and finally in the 1870s as Carlton Street. Thomas Street became Linden Lane, later Lombard Place. Or perhaps the map has them in the wrong order, and Emigrant Place became Linden Lane. That would explain why the correspondent to the *Herald* in 1851 referred to Linden Lane as London-Lane—in many places it is spelt 'Lindon'. In any case, by 1851 there were still two lanes running off Parramatta Street. London-Lane, the correspondent claimed, was 'a narrow dirty thoroughfare of thirty-two wooden houses', so bad that many were without tenants because 'the lane has become so notorious that it is shunned by all who can do so'. The houses contained two small rooms apiece and rented for two shillings a week. Dalton Street he

---

35 ANU/ NBAC Tooths, Z223, Box 6; James Broadbent, 'The Push East . . .' in Max Kelly (ed), *Sydney City of Suburbs* (1987), p 21.
36 Phillip Coleman Williams, 'Reminiscences of Old Sydney', *Descent*, Vol 16, p 19.

found to be 'in every respect superior', the houses having three rooms each and renting at 3/6 a week, but all were very cramped and unhealthy, a fact he found difficult to explain, as there was ample space around these streets, which could have housed hundreds of people.[37]

It is said that Cooper built his cottages as an inducement to his workers, to whom they were let, to vote for him in the elections held in 1843 for the newly reformed Legislative Council. If this was his aim he was spectacularly unsuccessful, coming bottom of the poll, and it could be argued that the quality of the houses might well have induced their inhabitants to vote for any candidate but Cooper. More importantly, his cause was not helped to a vicious campaign waged against him in the conservative press. There were many reasons why the local establishment was opposed to this emancipist, 'this vulgar, unlettered man' who put himself forward as 'the friend of the people', but there were also quite specific complaints against him in 1843, and these related directly to Cooper's building activities in Chippendale.

Robert Cooper, early manufacturer, developer and 'character'—a cheerful intelligent man ... or 'a bloated lump of flesh'.

For many people in Sydney, 1843 was not a good year. Urban unemployment was high enough to induce the appointment of a Select Committee on Distressed Labourers; men such as Cooper found it difficult to call in their creditors, and insolvencies were commonplace. By early 1843 banks began to fail. At this time, in this climate, Robert Cooper chose to build his cottages, to take advantage of cheap construction and labouring rates. However, by May it appears that Cooper realised he had overstretched himself and tried to end the contract. When Lynch and Hollingdale, the builders, declined to end it, Cooper attempted to bring two charges of felony against them. The charges, for theft of building materials, were considered mischievous, and were thrown out of court. Several days after this, an incensed Cooper ordered the men's dray and horses to be impounded, but Lynch, having established that it was his, drove it back. In this manoeuvre, the dray contained some timber, so Cooper's next move was to have Lynch taken into custody for stealing the timber, but although he was locked up 'a considerable time', Cooper failed to lay charges. Commenting on this incident, the Attorney-General claimed he 'never remembered any case which 'manifested such an entire disregard of the liberty of a fellow citizen'.

Lynch sued Cooper to obtain compensation for false imprisonment, and this case was conducted with liberal references to the preceding cases. It was contended that Cooper,

---

37 *SMH*, 8 March 1851.

unable to pay the builders, was desperate to have them 'lagged' in order to evade the contract. Justice Stephen, who heard the case in the Supreme Court, advised the jury that Lynch was entitled to compensation, and that 'if it appeared that the aggressor was actuated by a malicious or vindictive feeling, then the Jury could give exemplary damages.' He pointed out that not only was felony a serious crime, but in the case of Lynch it could lead to transportation. The implications of Cooper, himself an emancipist, inflicting this punishment through trumped-up charges would not have been lost on the jury. The judge's advice that 'they would act wisely by teaching him [Cooper] to regard the liberty and character of others', was heeded, and Lynch was awarded £100—enough to buy several blocks of Chippendale land in the depression of 1843.

All this occurred in May. The *Herald* gave the case wide coverage, claiming it was prepared to 'pollute' its pages with details of Cooper's doings only to 'prevent the irretrievable disgrace which the City would be subjected to were he to be elected'. He was not. In August, a few days after the first elected Legislative Council sat, Cooper declared himself insolvent. The ability to do this had only existed since the previous year, and had been introduced as an emergency measure to tide men of substance over the depression. It could also be used by the less scrupulous to hide their real assets and avoid their debts. In the *Herald*'s view, Cooper became insolvent 'for the mere purpose of avoiding payment of the claims of Lynch and Hollingdale'.[38]

The 1850s saw additional cramming in this area, so that there were soon two more lanes, Greens (or Grieves) and Charles (later Balfour). In all, there were about ninety cottages by the end of the fifties, all of them badly drained and of indifferent quality, according to the Inspector General of Police.[39]

Here too, next to these lanes, between them and the distillery, was St Benedict's Chapel and schoolhouse, which began dispensing moral and textbook education to the children of Chippendale from 1838. In July 1845 Archbishop Polding laid the foundation stone on this site for Sydney's second Roman Catholic Church and in 1856 the building was completed with the addition of a spire.[40] It was the grandest thing in Chippendale and stood in stark contrast to the cottages of its Irish-descended parishioners nearby.

Had you chosen to walk along Linden Lane or any of these lanes at mid-century, away from Parramatta Street, you would have come to a high wall at the end of it, broken down in places to allow passage into the paddocks beyond. The line of this wall, built by Cooper around the whole of his property, is delineated on the map. The wall was a rubble-stone construction, about twelve feet high and twenty inches thick, and ran along Parramatta Street to the boundary of St Benedict's. Here it sloped towards Abercrombie Place, narrowing the church's property to a triangle. It went right across Abercrombie Place, where it was later broken down as the street began to be formed:

38 R.L. Knight, 'Cooper, Robert', *ADB*, op.cit.; *SMH*, 24 May, 12 June, 1 September 1843.
39 Select Committee, 'Condition of the Working Classes of the Metropolis', *NSW V&P, LA*, 1859–60, Vol 4, p 1361.
40 Frank Clune, *Saga of Sydney*, pp 162–63.

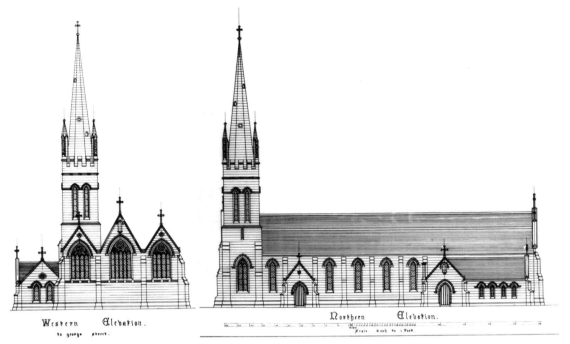

Western Elevation.
To george street.

Northern Elevation.
Scale inch to i foot.

St Benedict's Church. Note that the elevation labels are incorrect. The left hand drawing is the northern elevation, the right hand one is the western.

> It must have been originally built right across that street, as there were evidences of a break in the wall, and continued across the bottom of Carlton-street, then called Dalton's-lane; thence along across Linden's-lane, across Charles-street, now called Balfour-street, right up to Tooth's Brewery wall. There was evidence of the wall having been broken down at each of the lanes and streets named.[41]

It would seem that Cooper was not pleased with the development of Abercrombie Place as a main thoroughfare, because when he built a row of houses behind these lanes, parallel to Parramatta Street, he constructed several of them in such a way as to narrow off Abercrombie Place. It was probably also Cooper who erected a toll gate across the road near his bridge crossing the Blackwattle Creek. The bridge was necessary to prevent fouling the water, but it did encourage use of the road. To minimise this, there was a charge of a halfpenny for each person, a farthing for a sheep, twopence for a horse and threepence for a cart. This, according to M.J. Conlon, who remembered the toll being there in the 1850s, 'was hard on those attending St Benedict's Church and School. They had to pay if they lived at Chippendale . . . A great number, however, went round by Kensington Street, to avoid the toll'.[42] What with this toll, the bar on George Street going into town, and the imposing walls of the distillery and brewery, Chippendale's residents must have felt somewhat hemmed in, although open spaces were still prevalent in the area.

41 'Old Chum', 12 June 1910.
42 Ibid.

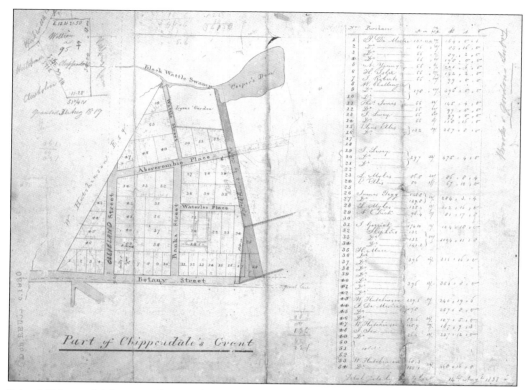

Sale of Chippendale's grant, 1838. Bank Street became the nucleus of this subdivision. Note that Cleveland Street stops at Abercrombie Place.

When Conlon referred to people living 'at Chippendale', he meant on the old Chippendale Estate behind Cooper's southern boundary, between Abercrombie Place and Botany Street (now Regent Street) which had been sold to Solomon Levey in 1821 and subdivided in August 1838. According to the selling agents, 'this most splendid estate' was well located, 'lively and picturesque in the extreme, having perfect panoramic views around, as well as being most salubriously situated for health'.[43] Which only goes to show that some people will say anything in order to make a sale. Chippendale was not lovely. It commanded no stunning views and attracted no wealthy residents to its vicinity. It did not feature in travellers' descriptions of Sydney, and it received scant attention from the chroniclers of Sydney's early development. Tales of grand houses and fine estates later subdivided into urban blocks do not feature in its history.

The sale was a tolerable success although not all the land was cleared. The smallest blocks had 66 foot frontages to Cleveland, Botany and Banks (now Meagher) streets. Others, towards Lyons Garden near Cooper's Dam, were larger. The highest prices were paid for the corner blocks on Cleveland and Botany streets, and the buyers included some

---

43 *Catalogue of Fifty Four allotments of land The property of the Late Solomon Levey Esq . . .* (J. Tegg and Co, Sydney, August 1838); LTO Deed Packet 1236, Document 4 lists Levey's properties.

Cottages in Elim Place, some of the best that Cooper built, have survived 150 years. In 2000 they became heritage listed.

old-time investors in Chippendale, like Hutchinson and Shepherd and Prosper de Mestre, who owned many houses in Sydney, and no doubt intended to extend his landlording activities to Chippendale.[44] One buyer was James Tegg, who subsequently left his mark on the area in the form of Tegg's Row, a mean row of eight wooden houses with three rooms each which appear in the city's Assessment Books by 1855 and had become decrepit enough to be demolished by 1882. Interestingly, Tegg was the printer of the catalogue for this sale, but if he was persuaded by its claims for 'this most splendid estate' his own contribution to Chippendale's development did not enhance the status of the area.

The streets of this subdivision gradually filled up in the 1840s. Banks Street, at the centre of the area, grew into a small commercial nucleus, with one shop and three houses in 1845, but six shops, twenty-seven houses and one hotel by 1848. By 1850 it contained more shops, including a butcher's, a grocer, John Mellon's Chippendale Hotel and Mrs Yarrington, who would make you a straw bonnet. The external streets, Cleveland Street and Botany Street, were more residential with some good quality houses, especially in Botany Street, where they ranged in value from five pounds per annum for some wooden, shingled, two room cottages, to sixty-five pounds for a two storey, eight-roomed house. Along with five others in Botany Street, this house had a coach house and stables in 1848, while by 1855 the Assessment Books record that Lawrence Miles, the owner, had further upgraded the property. Now described as having nine rooms with a slate roof in place of shingle, it boasted a coach house, servants' room and washhouse, and was valued at £150. In 1850 it

---

44 A list of purchasers is attached to map 'Part of Chippendale's grant, total sold by A Polack', 14 August 1838. Held in ML (Z M2 811. 1838/1).

1850. Large tracts of unsubdivided land still run through the centre of Chippendale—mostly Shepherd's and Cooper's. The rows of tiny cottages are clearly marked, including Cooper's Row which partially straddles Abercrombie Place. Cooper's other housing is on Parramatta Street, west of the Distillery, and on Cooks River Road, near Shepherd's Darling House.

was rented to James Martin, a solicitor and member of the Legislative Council who subsequently became Chief Justice of New South Wales. But this standard of housing was not common, and most of Martin's neighbours were less prosperous than himself. In the new streets of the estate, like Waterloo and Queen streets, Chippen and Dale streets, and the one squeezed between them, called Middle Street, small two or three room houses were the order of the day. Many of them were wooden and as lacking in imagination as the names of the streets they graced. Other streets in the area, such as Henrietta, had not appeared in the Assessment Books by mid-century, or else they were listed merely as buildings—Dick's Buildings, for instance, running back from Dale Street, but not yet in a sufficiently formed state to warrant a street title of their own.[45] Abercrombie Place had attracted only a few houses by 1850 but, in addition to the flour mill, held the Chippendale Academy, where local children were introduced to 'the noble science of geometry' and the wonders of 'elucidating by algebraic solution various problems of Euclid', if the advertisement of John and Marian Armstrong, who ran the school, is to be believed.[46]

With the exception of the wealthy of Botany Street, and the publicans and retailers serving local needs, this area would have been inhabited by the families of men who worked at the brewery. So too would Kensington Street, adjoining the brewery's northern perimeter. Today the brewery wall forms one side of this street, while on the other, a few old cottages still remain. In 1850 the street contained a mixture of houses, most of only two rooms. In addition to brewery workers, this street was the home of several butchers who probably worked at the Swamp Abattoirs across the Parramatta Road.

Other early cottages in Chippendale were those built on Parramatta Street and twenty-two stone cottages off Cooks River Road, close to the quarries which Cooper had excavated to build his factory and to increase the capacity of his dam. It is possible that the six cottages in Elim Place, each four roomed, had been there since about 1830, but the rest, in an unnamed street running parallel to Elim Place, came later. In the 1845 Assessment Books, there were twelve of these built and recorded as 'Cooper's cottages'. These were being erected in 1843, along with another 'thirty or forty' according to a newspaper report, being built parallel to Parramatta Street, running from the distillery to the brewery wall and straddling Abercrombie Street. By 1845 there were 55 cottages here (see map page 21) suggesting that those in excess of 'thirty or forty' may have been older stock. The assessors did not recognise this as a street, but regarded it as part of the distillery property. It was known as Cooper's Row, or Cooper's Rookery. It was this row of cottages which jutted into Abercrombie Place, narrowing its width. Each house was of two rooms, with a twelve foot frontage, on blocks of land only thirty-seven feet deep. They were built of wood, with shingled roofs, and were notoriously bad.

It seems that the new cottages off Cooks River Road may not have been finished for some time, or if they were, they did not easily find tenants, because according to the 1845

---

45 This description is based on information found in the City Council's Assessment Books 1845–55 and in *Ford's Sydney Directory*, 1851. Incidentally, Chippen, Middle and Dale streets subsequently became Chippen, Dale and Balfour streets, in that order.
46 *SMH*, 7 October 1844.

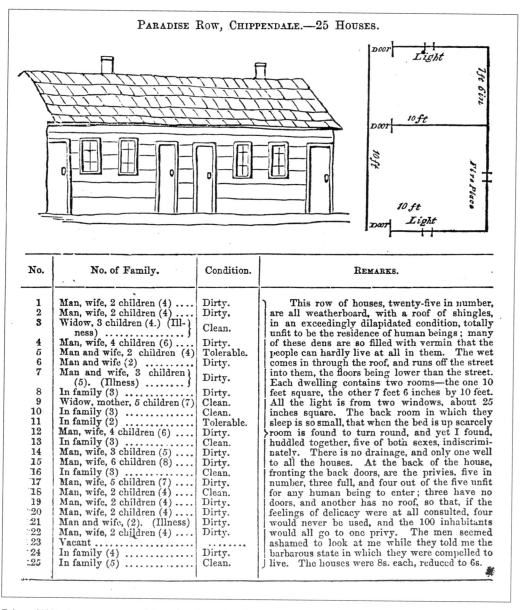

PARADISE ROW, CHIPPENDALE.—25 HOUSES.

No.	No. of Family.	Condition.	REMARKS.
1	Man, wife, 2 children (4)	Dirty.	This row of houses, twenty-five in number, are all weatherboard, with a roof of shingles, in an exceedingly dilapidated condition, totally unfit to be the residence of human beings; many of these dens are so filled with vermin that the people can hardly live at all in them. The wet comes in through the roof, and runs off the street into them, the floors being lower than the street. Each dwelling contains two rooms—the one 10 feet square, the other 7 feet 6 inches by 10 feet. All the light is from two windows, about 25 inches square. The back room in which they sleep is so small, that when the bed is up scarcely room is found to turn round, and yet I found, huddled together, five of both sexes, indiscriminately. There is no drainage, and only one well to all the houses. At the back of the house, fronting the back doors, are the privies, five in number, three full, and four out of the five unfit for any human being to enter; three have no doors, and another has no roof, so that, if the feelings of delicacy were at all consulted, four would never be used, and the 100 inhabitants would all go to one privy. The men seemed ashamed to look at me while they told me the barbarous state in which they were compelled to live. The houses were 8s. each, reduced to 6s.
2	Man, wife, 2 children (4)	Dirty.	
3	Widow, 3 children (4.) (Illness)	Clean.	
4	Man, wife, 4 children (6)	Dirty.	
5	Man and wife, 2 children (4)	Tolerable.	
6	Man and wife (2)	Dirty.	
7	Man and wife, 3 children (5). (Illness)	Dirty.	
8	In family (3)	Dirty.	
9	Widow, mother, 5 children (7)	Clean.	
10	In family (3)	Clean.	
11	In family (2)	Tolerable.	
12	Man, wife, 4 children (6)	Dirty.	
13	In family (3)	Clean.	
14	Man, wife, 3 children (5)	Dirty.	
15	Man, wife, 6 children (8)	Dirty.	
16	In family (3)	Clean.	
17	Man, wife, 5 children (7)	Dirty.	
18	Man, wife, 2 children (4)	Clean.	
19	Man, wife, 2 children (4)	Dirty.	
20	Man, wife, 2 children (4)	Dirty.	
21	Man and wife, (2). (Illness)	Dirty.	
22	Man, wife, 2 children (4)	Dirty.	
23	Vacant	....	
24	In family (4)	Dirty.	
25	In family (5)	Clean.	

Edward Wise's assessment of Paradise Row (Smithers Street).

Assessment Books, none was occupied. A few in Cooper's Row also stood empty. However, against these the assessor had written 'dilapidated', which strengthens the case for some of them being older than 1843. All were owned by the Union Bank of Australia. The stamp of Robert Cooper was firmly upon the face of Chippendale, but in truth his hold was tenuous. So too was the hold of these cottages. By 1851 some had been washed away in a flood, while 'about one-fourth of the rest have fallen out of the perpendicular, and are propped up by gables fixed in the ground. Those that despise the upright ways of their neighbours are uninhabited; they are all unsafe to live in'.[47]

The accuracy of this description was confirmed by the vivid recollections of M.J. Conlon sixty years later:

> *The row of cottages, before the gold era, let for about two shillings a week each, and it was astonishing what a number of families crouched into these small cribs. It seems, in those days, to be a ruling passion with builders to erect small houses, on a sort of dog kennel plan. About the year 1850 a great fall of rain occurred, and Waterloo-street and Wellington-street, Chippendale, became flooded. It was on a Sunday, and the waters broke through a gateway in Wellington-street and swept away the foundations of three of the end houses in Cooper's Row, and leveling the buildings, they were never restored. A little further south, on another occasion, seven fell from sheer decay.*[48]

This kind of barracks accommodation, of timber and shingle construction, was repeated many times elsewhere in Chippendale, most of it constructed in the 1840s. Conlon recalled that there were 'some hundreds around the neighbourhood'. In addition to Tegg's and Cooper's Rows there was Paradise Row, owned by Thomas Broughton, who was Mayor of Sydney in 1846, and who owned vast tracts of urban land. This row of houses so offended Edward Wise, the Attorney-General, that when he was giving evidence to the select committee 'on the condition of the working classes' in 1859, he submitted a sketch of these buildings, with detailed notes attached. The fifty rooms of the twenty-five houses accommodated 103 people, without either comfort or decorum, as his report makes clear. This select committee had been set up to investigate social conditions in Sydney generated by the chaotic urban explosion of the gold rush decade, but Paradise Row clearly predated these events.[49] There are many tales of housing shortages in the 1850s resulting in makeshift and jerry-built houses, but the Chippendale rows were a response to the depression of the 40s, not the housing pressures of the 50s. W.S. Jevons, whom we will meet again in Chapter 2, described Linden Lane in 1858, with its tiny two-roomed weatherboard rows of cottages, as 'a shocking sight . . . quite uniform and uniformly abominable throughout'.[50] The select committee also singled out the area just north of the brewery for negative comment. Dr Graham, the City Health Officer, described the houses in Kensington Street as being 'in a most wretched condition, so far as ventilation and cleanliness are concerned'.[51] Other streets in this area were also criticised.

This then was Chippendale at mid-century. Parramatta Street, the area's face to the rest of Sydney, was lined with a jumble of residential and commercial buildings, just under one hundred of each. Small scale industrial activity associated with the market trade—forges, harness makers and so on—was encouraged here because of its location outside the toll

47 *SMH*, 8 March 1851.
48 'Old Chum', 26 June 1910
49 SC 'Condition of the Working Classes . . .', op. cit. p 1320.
50 W.S. Jevons, 'Social Survey of Australian Cities, 1858', ML MS B864.
51 SC 'Condition of the Working Classes . . .', op. cit. p 1315.

gate at the top of George Street. Most of the buildings were of two storeys, but many contained only two rooms. Shingles dominated and the vast majority of the buildings were rented rather than owner occupied. Public houses, ten in all on the Chippendale side alone, were larger, usually containing eight or ten rooms, and a few were built of stone, possibly from Cooper's quarry, possibly from Pyrmont. The term 'shop' in this vicinity often meant nothing more than a stall or a counter in the front room of a hovel where assorted goods were exchanged or sold, or rotted for lack of customers. Phillip Whalan's ginger beer factory, as we have seen, was a mere skillion attached to a wooden stable—a very low key affair valued at five pounds when even the houses in the same area ranged from nine pounds up to fifteen pounds. The number of people living in and behind this commercial road who gave their occupation as 'dealer' indicates the ephemeral nature of much of the business activity carried on. Goods acquired legally or illegally changed hands for rock bottom prices over counters and down alleyways, plans and deals were hatched over jugs of Cooper's gin or Tooth's ale in corner pubs, or outside St Benedict's after a well attended mass on Sunday morning. Many men would have oscillated between petty trafficking of this sort and labouring jobs in the local industrial plants which generated casual and seasonal labour. In the streets and lanes the accents of working class London and Dublin were heard in the spaces between the rumbling of carts and complaining of animals being driven to the abattoirs across the road. Depending on the wind direction, the area was heavy with odours of these abattoirs or with the smell of hops from the brewery. The streets lay thick with dust in dry weather, while on wet days John Armstrong closed his school for lack of pupils, as rivulets draining the area turned it into a bog.

Behind all this, where the creek ran into the dam, there were still green places and remnants of watercress fields, but these were being encroached on from the west by housing on Chippendale's original grant. The waterway, so important in attracting settlement initially, would continue to be crucial to Chippendale's development in the following decades, but its role would gradually change. What was a natural bounty would gradually become an environmental problem, and eventually contribute to a residential disaster.

2

FROM 1850 TO 1880

Y MID-CENTURY Chippendale was still at the end of town, and far from being built
out. Carters Barracks had only recently been emptied of convicts and handed over
to the two main religious denominations to use as refuges for poor and 'fallen' women. The
Anglican 'Sydney Female Refuge' and the Roman Catholic 'House of the Good Samaritan',
along with the longstanding Benevolent Asylum, made a striking statement about the
pitfalls and hardships of colonial life. Sydney had recently experienced a number of years
of severe depression when the growth of the town had slowed, and the toll gate and police
station at the end of George Street still symbolised the town boundary. In fact, the
incorporation of the city in 1842 had placed Chippendale just with its jurisdiction, with
two of its main streets, Newtown Road and Cleveland Street, forming the south-west
corner of the city. But the new city corporation, struggling with a lack of funds and
expertise, rarely allowed its thoughts of town improvements to wander as far afield as
Chippendale. Far more central and built-up locations were crying out for basic amentities,
such as roads and light and water, and in the municipal mind Chippendale seemed far
away. The inhabitants were first assessed in order for the corporation to levy rates in 1845,
but the problems were many and the rates did not stretch very far. Parramatta Street was

The Benevolent Asylum—one of a cluster of charity buildings on the road to Chippendale.

Chippendale c. 1855, from the University. The road through the centre of the illustration is Newtown Road (Cooks River Road), with Shepherd's Darling Nursery and house on right. The centre smoke stack is the distillery/refinery and the large square tower the brewery. Note that the toll gate has moved out to the corner of Newtown Road and Parramatta Street and that the lake is being used to wash down the horses before the haul into town.

still the location for cattleyards, slaughterhouses, ramshackle stores and rowdy public houses, and was still thought of as beyond the city. Even as late as 1858, the *Sydney Morning Herald* was unaware or had forgotten that Chippendale was part of the city. In an article berating citizens for not showing more enthusiasm for the new suburban Municipalities Act, it observed that if people wished to go on 'enjoying the plenitude of effluvia' and 'pick their way through puddles and stumbling blocks', then that was their lookout. In the list of 'suburbs' which suffered these qualities, it included Chippendale.[1] But alas Chippendale could not incorporate, being within the boundaries of Sydney. The newspaper's mistake was one which many citizens would have made at the time.

However, by then, 1858, Chippendale was much more built up than at the midpoint of the century. The previous year the fledgling Sydney University had moved from temporary premises in the Sydney College to its new building on what had been Grose Farm, on the other side of Newtown Road from Chippendale. Trains had been running from the original Redfern station behind Chippendale for more than two years. And, most significantly of all, the impact of the gold rushes had radically altered the face of Sydney.

The discovery of gold in 1851 signalled the beginning of several years of enormous social disruption. Men and women, especially men, simply downed tools and walked away from dull or unrewarding lives in search of adventure and wealth. In the second half of May, business on Parramatta Street was brisk as horses were shod and carts knocked into shape for the first contingent beginning the trek to Bathurst. Many simply headed out of

---

1 Quoted in F. A. Larcombe, *The Origin Of Local Government in NSW*, Vol 1 (1973), p 267.

town on foot. The police at the station at the beginning of the street were kept busy interrogating travellers and attempting to return those who were indentured or bonded and not free to be leaving town, but the rush was too great and they were unequal to the task. Social chaos reigned.

At the same time, pressure on existing resources increased enormously as people flocked to ports such as Sydney to join in the stampede. Prices of food and accommodation soared, and jerry-built cottages sprang up all over the town's outskirts, including Chippendale. Not that poorly constructed houses were a new phenomenon there. The two-roomed wooden cottages discussed in the last chapter which rented for two shillings a week before gold, earned twelve shillings a week in the six months after its discovery. Wages of labourers went from two-and-six a day to twenty-three shillings, and anyone who wanted it could get work, provided they were not fussy about the type of work.

E. W. KNOX, after half a century of sugar-refining.

E. W. Knox, Chairman of Directors, CSR 1855–1901.

But while gold would have an enormous impact on Chippendale, as it would everywhere, it was a different product which would become closely associated with the area's fortunes in the following decades. That product was sugar.

As we have already seen, Robert Cooper never really gained firm control of his Brisbane Distillery after 1850, and in 1852 he sold it to R.M. Robey, Clark Irving and Edward Knox, principals in the Australasian Sugar Company which had been manufacturing sugar in Sydney since 1842. All three men were free immigrants with considerable standing in the commercial world of Sydney, and considerable involvement in worthy social ventures. If Robert Cooper represented the first generation of colonial adventurers, these men represented a second generation of more respectable investors and merchants. Clark Irving had earlier had dealings with Cooper. These resulted in his obtaining a judgment against him in 1844 and a court order to sell his property. This had been prevented by Cooper agreeing to pay Irving a sum of money and to transfer to him land on the Kensington Estate, east of Kensington Street in Chippendale.[2]

The Brisbane Distillery was leased to the sugar company, which also had plants at Canterbury and in the city (the old Bowden's Sugar Refinery at the corner of Liverpool and Pitt streets). When it became difficult to work the Canterbury refinery for want of labour in 1852, activities were gradually concentrated in Sydney. Seventy men were employed at Canterbury in 1851 and only twenty-nine in Sydney. Twelve months later, with numbers down, the balance had moved in favour of Sydney, with twenty-seven at Canterbury and forty-two in Sydney. The wages sheets of the company indicate that early employment in Chippendale was limited to a few hands, but by 1854, with demand and prices for sugar

2 LTO Document 988, Book 10: Indenture between Robert Cooper and Robert William Newman and Clark Irving.

high, it was decided to rebuild and refit the Brisbane Sugar House, as it was called. During 1853 about ten people, including some of the company's engineers, were employed at Chippendale, while the wages sheet for February 1854 shows the first real concentration of workers here. The 54 names listed reduce to 45, once double counting is eliminated. The appearance of the same names twice suggests that the engineers and carpenters were splitting their time between the old and new plants as pressure was increased to finish off the refurbishing of the Chippendale works. Labour was scarce, and the company was paying twenty-seven shillings a day for stone masons and eighteen shillings for carpenters. Before the discovery of gold, seven or eight shillings would have bought the same labour. Some of the senior employees were working round the clock, like the engineer Boag, who took home £6, but had worked the equivalent of two full days' overtime on top of a six-day, ten-hour-a-day week. Poolman, who was probably supervising the operation, had worked the equivalent of just over eight days, probably at odd hours.[3] Overtime, it is noted, was paid for at the same rate as regular hours of work.

In the same year, 1854, for reasons which did not impinge on the oprations of the firm in Chippendale, the Australasian Sugar Company was dissolved and the property sold to the Colonial Sugar Refining Company, newly formed in 1855, for £120,000.[4] The CSR, like its predecessor, was always referred to in common parlance as simply the Sugar Company. The original owners continued to be represented in the new firm, with Edward Knox becoming principal shareholder and director of the company, while Robey's brother, James, became manager of the sugar house. In the city's Assessment Books, these names appear as owners of the various properties previously belonging to Cooper and his banks, and eventually streets came to be known by the names of these new Chippendale employers. Brisbane Street, named for the Brisbane distillery and the governor, became Knox Street by the mid-1870s, Irving Street made its appearance (and has since gone again), while the infamous Cooper's Rookery, elevated to the title of Cooper's Row in 1848, briefly became Robey's Row in 1855.

In that year, the Colonial Sugar Refining Company demolished most of the cottages in this area, some of which therefore had a life's span of only ten years. In their place they built more substantial four-roomed, two storey brick houses with slate roofs. It would seem that the refinery did not intend to use them as tied cottages, but to sell them off to private interests. In a bid to increase profits, they requested that the city corporation make roads in the area, which until now had been just a paddock full of hovels at the back of the old distillery dam. A map drawn to persuade the Council to do this shows two streets in this area running off Abercrombie Street—one called Cooper and one called Robey Street.[5]

In fact there was as yet only one street, the one hitherto called Cooper's, but in the 1855 Assessment Book this is called Robey's Row. By the next assessment the street had reverted to being Cooper's Row, and many people in Chippendale and the whole of Sydney could

3 ANU/NBAC, CSR, Z303, A1.0.1, Document 1, E. R. Day, unpublished notes on CSR c. 1949.
4 CSR (Syd), A.5.0.8, Document 2.
5 'The Estate of the Colonial Sugar Refining Company, Parramatta Street, applied for by trustees...Syd.' (c.1855), map, ML.

have told you why. The Robey brothers had disagreed with other directors of the company, and in 1857 James Robey was sacked when it was learned that he intended to set up a rival company. This duly occurred, the new establishment on the North Shore at Oyster Cove being called the New Sugar Works and Refinery. As a parting shot at the Company, Robey threatened to dissolve it and caused an uproar by inserting notices in the press announcing the dissolution. In fact this was not to happen, and instead the Company moved into a period of expansion and consolidation, buying out its competitors, including Robey, in 1859. In this venture, it probably received some help from Irving's manipulations of the Australian Joint Stock Bank, where both he and Robey were directors. The bank curtailed Robey's credit, allegedly on Irving's recommendation, forcing Robey to sell out at a loss to CSR. The two men engaged in a bitter pamphlet war and much litigation thereafter.[6]

The name Cooper's Row probably reflected the growing interest in the area of Daniel Cooper (later Sir Daniel, a well known Sydney merchant and politician), no relation to Robert. Daniel Cooper was an original shareholder in CSR and a trustee and chairman of the board from 1857 to 1859. This may explain why part of the street is currently called Daniel's Street. This Cooper was the nephew of Daniel Cooper who had been a business partner of Solomon Levey, whom we have already met as a landholder in Chippendale. At his uncle's death, Daniel Cooper the younger inherited much of his Sydney property.[7] He was represented on the board of Tooths Brewery, and the Tooths were original shareholders in CSR in the 1850s. When Edward Knox was looking for somewhere to live while temporarily in London in 1878, he and his family stayed at Robert Tooth's London apartment.[8] The commercial interests of these wealthy families with business affairs in Chippendale became inevitably intermeshed.

The establishment of the refinery in Chippendale meant more stable employment in the area. After the formation of the new company, work resumed on 1 January 1855 with new machinery imported in 1854. There were four 30 horsepower steam boilers, two vacuum pans which each held about 30 hundredweight of sugar crystals and syrup, and six small centrifugal machines which dried the sugar. These operations produced about 120 tons of sugar per week and employed seventy or eighty men. In addition fifteen to twenty horses and drays hauled the raw product and the coal required for fuel from the company's store at Campbell's wharf, Circular Quay, up through town to Chippendale.[9] Its annual production of about 6000 tons represented about one third of the colony's consumption of sugar, according to an interested party, who informed a colleague in Batavia that:

> *The Company is making a bold effort now to get into its hands the whole of the Import trade in Raw Sugars of New South Wales and in this way they hope to enjoy the Monopoly of Supplying the entire consumption of the Colony—say 18,000 Tons annually.*

---

6 Louise T. Daley, 'Irving, Clark (1808–1865)', *ADB*, Vol. 4, 1966, p 462; Suzanne Edgar, 'Robey, Ralph Mayer (1809–1864); *ADB*, Vol. 6, 1966, pp 47, 48.

7 A.W. Martin, 'Cooper, Sir. Daniel (1821–1902)', *ADB*, Vol. 3, 1966, p 452.

8 Sir E. Knox, Autobiographical Notes, typescript, ML.

9 ANU/NBAC.CSR, E. R. Day notes, chapter 11.

Colonial Sugar Refinery, c.1860.

This report went on to say that achieving monopoly was unlikely and that production in the East Indies would be able to undercut them.[10] Profits were uncertain, and it was likely that the production of rum, distilled from the molasses which resulted from the sugar-refining process, would be the profitable part of the operation and important for at least the first decade after 1855. The plant could produce 3000 gallons a week, and rum enjoyed a more certain market price than sugar in the early days.[11]

However, not only did the company eventually achieve a refining monopoly and move into sugar cane production as well, but the growing popularity and consumption of cane sugar as the nineteenth century progressed ensured that output and employment at the refinery would burgeon. By 1878, when the Chippendale site was abandoned in favour of Pyrmont, weekly production had risen from about one hundred tons to 240 tons, and by the end of the century, the weekly output exceeded 1000 tons.[12]

With increasing production came not only increasing employment, but increasing environmental pollution. There were two main sources. The first arose from the company's practice of burning bones to create charcoal for filtering purposes. The second source was the old Cooper's Dam. In the refining process, large amounts of water were needed for condensing purposes, and as this water was merely reticulated through the plant and never came in contact with the sugar, its purity or lack of it was not crucial. At various times the dam water was used for this purpose, but as settlement came closer the water became more foul and the nuisance grew.

---

10 ANU/NBAC.CSR, Z303, A.1.0.1, Document 47, Private memo for Alex Fraser, Esq., Batavia, August 1855.
11 Ibid.
12 ANU/NBAC.CSR, E. R. Day notes, pp 7–9.

The first problem, that of burning bones for charcoal, reached a crisis point in October 1870 when the City Council began receiving formal petitions against this process from residents. One petition complained of 'a poisonous matter . . . thrown off in a liquid state and also as a vapour infecting the purity of the atmosphere . . . The growing trade of the Company only increases the danger and nuisances', and hoped the Council would act to suppress this 'gigantic nuisance'. Residents in the adjoining suburb of Glebe complained that 'bones in every stage of decomposition' were stacked high on the premises, and that 'the effluvia, Gas and Smoke generated by the storing and burning of said bones are in the highest degree prejudicial to health, obnoxious and offensive in the extreme and detrimental to the social advancement of the district.' This same petition was also received from residents of Parramatta Street and Chippendale, residents of South Sydney and Shepherds Paddock.[13]

Dr Frederick Dansey, the City Health Officer, duly visited the site and reported on it to the Mayor. He estimated that there were 300 tons of 'stinking bones' lying about and also observed that the old dam was in a bad state.[14] Thus began years of bad relations between the City Council and the CSR Company over the problems of charcoal production and the state of the waterway.

Around this time the Company stopped using the dam's water for condensation, allowed the dam to silt up, and began using mains water instead. This, of course, was much more acceptable environmentally, but it placed the Council in a dilemma. Clearly the company was doing the right thing by Chippendale residents, who ought to have been the Council's first concern, but in fact the water could only be supplied to the Sugar Company by curtailing supplies to the residents of The Glebe. The solution to this problem was to lay extra pipes, but the Council did not have the funds. Each year demands on the main which supplied The Glebe and also the refinery were growing, because there were more houses to supply and because the refinery's output was increasing. At the same time the source of the supply, a series of dams built on the Botany Swamps, was yielding less water.

In response to this problem, the company was formally notified in March 1872 that from then on their water consumption would be metered, which would result in steeper charges. The motives for this were probably twofold: to encourage lower consumption and to recover revenue in line with the amount of water being used. Edgar Ross, manager of the company, wrote a swift reply, claiming that the refinery already paid more for water than anyone else in Sydney, and threatening to close the works down. Furthermore, he said, the company used the water over and over again, letting it run away when its condition became 'unfit for further use'. The only way they could reduce consumption would be by holding it in a reservoir, which would create a nuisance. This obvious reference to the bad old days of using Cooper's Dam water was emphasised by pointing out that the Company believed the City Council owed it some favours since the Council had allowed refuse and sewage to enter the dam, making its water unfit for industrial use.[15] Ross's suggestion that production

---

13 NSCA CRS 26/106/1044, October 1870.
14 NSCA CRS 26/106/1052, CHO to Mayor, 2 November 1870.
15 CRS 26/114/257, CSR to Mayor 14 March 1872.

might end was mere bluff. Production was healthy, and the company's records show rising profits from the mid-1860s.[16] A second implied threat, of reactivating the old dam, was swiftly acted upon. In August of that year, Dr Dansey and Richard Seymour, the city's nuisance inspector, reported that the condition of the dam and the creek below it was 'offensive and sickening'. In the company's operations, the water was heated to quite high temperatures, which increased the level of odour, and when the dam level became too high, water was run off downstream, causing a nuisance. When the level of the dam fell, the exposed sides similarly exacerbated the problem.

The Company's response was to admit the nuisance, but not the responsibility. They had a legal right to the water in Blackwattle Creek, they said. This the Council accepted, and interestingly there was now no discussion of using town water as both parties knew it simply was not there in quantities sufficient for the refinery's needs. The Company blamed the Council for allowing the creek to become foul, and urged it to take action to prevent its pollution.[17] The Council already prosecuted offenders, Seymour assured the Mayor, but he pointed out that they could do nothing about problems which originated upstream of the city boundaries, in Redfern and Darlington. As well as containing high levels of suburban sewage, it received the run off from a cowyard and a pigsty and the industrial waste from a soap factory in Redfern.[18] This question, of limited boundaries and a rapidly growing city, was to create a multitude of problems for municipal control in metropolitan Sydney. In 1850, when most of the urban area was within the city boundary, it had not mattered. By 1870, it did. Consequently, talk of 'Greater Sydney' began in this decade.[19]

Following receipt of this report, the Mayor and aldermen ventured out to Chippendale to see and smell for themselves what their officers had reported. Tensions ran high late in 1872, and Seymour was instructed to prosecute various parties for fouling the stream, including the Colonial Sugar Refining Company.

The prosecution failed because the Sugar Company produced numbers of local residents who were prepared to vouch for the sweetness of the air in Chippendale. Whether these people were bribed, or afraid of losing their jobs or just immune to the finer details of their environment we will never know, but the Council officers, giving evidence to the Sewage and Health Board a few years later in 1876, had no doubts that their own assessment of the situation had not been exaggerated. Seymour said he had heard 'hundreds of persons' complain of the area, while Thomas Bradridge, the City Surveyor, declared emphatically that he 'would not live in the vicinity of those creeks'. 'We had only our own witnesses, who did not reside in the locality', said Seymour. 'There was such a balance of evidence on their side . . . and all residing in the locality, that we had no chance.'[20]

Having thus defended its good name in the eyes of the law, if not in the eyes (or noses)

16 ANU/NBAC.CSR, Z303, A1.0.1, E. R. Day notes, Appendix G.
17 NSCA CRS 26//116/719, CHO to Mayor, 5 August 1872; NSCA CRS 26/116//743, CSR to TC, 9 August 1872.
18 NSCA CRS 26/117/940, CHO and Inspector of Nuisances to Mayor, 22 October 1872.
19 For example, this was discussed at the Select Committee on the Working of Municipalites, *NSW V&P*, LA, 1873–4M, Vol 5, p 444.
20 SCSSHB, 6th Progress Report, *NSW V&P*, LA, 1875, Vol 5, p 444.

of the municipal officers or residents, the Sugar Company further consolidated its moral superiority by several times successfully prosecuting the soap manufacturer, Mulcahy's of Redfern. Soap refuse and grease 'had almost been taken to the Town Hall in barrow-loads', but the Council could not act to prosecute a factory beyond the city boundaries. The fact that the Sugar Company could was a method of thumbing its nose at the civic fathers. On the positive side, it also probably resulted in some cleansing of the creek. However, the claim of the Company's manager, Samuel Poolman, that after each prosecution the water became 'as pure as we could wish it to be' was unconvincing.[21] The concentration of settlement, and consequently, effluent, only increased.

After losing its court action against the Company, the Council considered diverting the Blackwattle Creek through the Abercrombie Street sewer, but legally they could not do so as it would have deprived the Company of its water rights. Similarly a proposal in 1874 to cover it—that is, to make a sewer through the company's property—foundered on legal grounds, because the Council's powers extended only to placing sewers in their own property which essentially limited it to the public streets.[22] The Sugar Company's refusal to co-operate was based on the knowledge that by now the Council could no longer supply them with water in any case.

By the mid-seventies, then, environmental conditions in Chippendale had deteriorated to the point where it was recognised as one of the most unhealthy localities in Sydney. The Council's records are a monument to the extent of the environmental degradation of the area, as well as to its own inaction. The slaughterhouses of earlier decades had officially been closed down when new public abattoirs were opened on Glebe Island in 1860, but a large number of butchers near Parramatta Street continued to slaughter illegally, adding offal and blood to the sewage and dairy run off entering the Blackwattle Swamp. If anything, the area just opposite Chippendale, in Ultimo, was more polluted, more damp underfoot and more poverty stricken than Chippendale itself, but there was not much to recommend either side of Parramatta Street. Dansey, the Health Officer, reported widespread fever in 1872 in the vicinity of Kensington Street, and he and Seymour wrote copious reports about the unpleasant state of the creek. Where Philip Coleman Williams recalled rowing a boat under Parramatta Street at mid-century, the creek was now referred to as a 'culvert' passing under the road, used in 1873 'by the "busmen and boys as a [water] closet and . . . in a most disgusting and filthy state"'.[23] After this, the Council constantly employed staff to clear out the creek at this bridge and at the point of entry into Blackwattle Swamp, but the only realistic solution, that of adequate sewage, had proved too great an engineering and financial undertaking to contemplate seriously. In a few short decades 'civilisation' had turned the well-watered pleasant land of Shepherd's Bush and Chippendale's farm into a mire.

---

21 Ibid, pp 441–42.
22 NSCA CRS 26/124/1019, City Engineer, 27 November 1873; NSCA//CRS 26/126/218, 219, CHO and Inspector of Nuisances 19 March 1874.
23 SCSSHB, 6th Progress Report, p 445; NSCA CRS 26/113/39, CHO, 16 January 1872; NSCA CRS 26/124/1011, CHO and Inspector of Nuisance, 24 November 1873.

As unrestrained, unplanned urban growth accelerated in the decades after the gold rushes, many areas experienced deteriorating living conditions. By 1875 an unconcerned colonial government had been sufficiently pressured by alarming health statistics and public outcry to agree to an investigation into public health issues, especially concerning the problems and shortcomings of the sewage system. The Sydney City and Suburban Sewage and Health Board was established in April. This Board delivered twelve lengthy and disturbing reports to the government about sewage, water supply, slaughtering, noxious trades and slum housing. And so serious a problem was the 'Sugar Company Creek' considered to be, that it was singled out for specific study and reported on at length.[24] The City Engineer, Francis Bell, and the City Health Officer, Dansey, were members of the Health Board committee that considered this problem. It documented the stalemate. The Company had acted legally within its rights, but the result was socially unacceptable. The Council was by and large powerless, but unhelpful. 'We find great difficulty in making any recommendation on this subject', reported the Board:

> The Company have an undoubted right to use of the water. It is not contaminated by them to any sensible extent, but the effects of the contamination arising from the occupation of the area drained by the upper part of the creek are to some extent aggravated by the nature of Company's operation . . .We can only recommend that the influence of the Government may be exerted to effect an arrangement under which the Company may use the city water exclusively, and that the sewage . . . be diverted, as suggested by Mr Bell, into the Abercrombie Street sewer.[25]

And so it was. Perhaps it was the adverse publicity which the Board's reports created which persuaded the Colonial Sugar Refining Company to notify the Town Clerk in July 1875 that they would give up their water right in exchange for an adequate cheap supply of town water. Fortuitously, extensions to the Botany works made supply a possibility, and as the water in the old Busby's Bore was no longer used, the city engineer recommended using it to clean out the dam, free of charge for six weeks, as suggested by the Board. Thereafter the Company was to be supplied with water from the Lachlan Swamps. A suggestion that the Company be granted cheap water rates, however, was rejected by the Council—after all, this was how the problem had started in the first place, with the Sugar Company declining to pay increased water rates.[26] The whole five year episode had not reflected well on either party.

What did not come out in this investigation was the fact that the Colonial Sugar Refining Company was considering vacating its Chippendale premises altogether. At the beginning of 1875 the Board of Directors had confirmed the truth of a rumour that an unknown potential rival was interested in a piece of land on the end of the Pyrmont Peninsula, and by the time the Health Board was admonishing them to clean up the Chippendale dam, the

---

24 See Shirley Fitzgerald, *Rising Damp* (1987), pp 82–85.

25 SCSSHB, 6th Progress Report, p 371.

26 NSCA/CRS 26/134/435, CSR to TC; CRS 26/134//418, 423, SCSSHB to TC.

Company was already negotiating to buy this land. The Company purchased the lease in September 1875.[27] So the offer to go onto town water was not so magnanimous, and the chance of getting the dam cleaned up with free water too good to pass up.

During 1876, probably as a result of further cleaning up of the old property, Chippendale's residents were again up in arms. It was alleged, and Richard Seymour confirmed, that they were burning 'sugar baskets and similar packages' behind the refinery early in the mornings with 'such a glare and column of smoke that it is surprising that the Fire Commissioners have not already taken notice of it'. The foul smell often woke residents up while the smoke 'blackened the curtains, bed, furniture and everything in the houses and has at length become an intolerable nuisance'. Seymour reported lamely that nothing could be done legally as the burning took place more than one hundred yards from any house, but he said the gentleman in charge would try to burn in smaller quantities. (Interestingly, the clerk at the City Council who filed the complaint put it under the heading 'Abercrombie Street/Bones burnt at Sugar Works'. It did not mention bones, and it is unlikely that the Company still practised this in Chippendale at this date, but presumably this activity was firmly linked with the company in the municipal mind.)[28]

Some of these problems were the inevitable result of the incompatability of heavy industry and close residential settlement, and no doubt the Sugar Company itself was anticipating more community acceptance when it moved to Pyrmont. The peninsula, although close to the city centre, was only sparsely populated. The water access for the ships the company was beginning to acquire was important, and initially it was hoped that an artesian well being sunk on the property would supply some of the refinery's needs. A report of this operation records that boring commenced in mid-January 1876, and on early evidence it was anticipated that twenty thousand to thirty thousand gallons of water per day would be released. This supply did not materialise, but clearly the water expenses of the company were sufficient to encourage this experiment.[29]

The move would have meant that many Chippendale men now had a longer walk to work, but it was not prohibitive, and the reduction in suffocating smells and blackened curtains would have been welcomed by their wives.

The new refinery commenced operations at the beginning of 1878. In the previous year, Edward Knox, the chairman of directors, made a personal gift of £1500 to his employees. The amount that each man received was calculated in relation to the rate of his pay and the number of years he had worked for the company, and as these calculations have been preserved they give us a good record of who was employed in Chippendale in the last year that sugar was refined there.[30] The list contains 129 names, of whom thirty were listed as 'engineers hands'. The rest would have been of various trades, and unskilled laborers. A description of jobs a few years later includes some skilled work such as pattern

---

27 ANU/NBAC, CSR, Z303, A1.0.2, Document 3, Extracts from Board Minutes.

28 NSCA CRS 26//139//368.

29 ANU/NBAC, CSR, Z303, A5.1.1, Document 5, 'Artesian Well for the Sugar Company', anon, 1876.

30 ANU/NBAC, CSR, Z303, A2.0.7, Document 8, Papers relating to Edward Knox's personal gift of £1500 to CSR employee 1877.

Kent Brewery Yard, c.1860–70 . . . top hats and cloth caps.

making and coopering, but most of the work was unskilled—drying sacks, sackmaking, grinding bones, cleaning out filters and vats.[31] Much of the work was done in hot moist conditions, wearing the minimum of clothing, and would have been exhausting. Of these 129 workers who received a bonus in 1877, ninety-two had commenced working at the refinery within the past seven years, fifty-six of them in the last three years. Only four men had twenty-five years or more employment to their credit. By today's standards this is a high turnover rate, and it probably was then too. Working in the refinery was not something one did if anything else could be found.

In 1877 a skilled worker got ten shillings and in a few cases twelve shillings a day, while labourers got seven shillings, and apprentices and messengers as little as one-and-eight. When Knox divided up his largesse, a lad named Lock, who earned two-and-six a day and had worked at the refinery for two years, received a bonus of one pound, while Baylis, a labourer of sixteen years' service at seven shillings a day, received eight guineas. T. Perigo, the only employee whose wage was quoted weekly, at five pounds, had been with the company since 1845, and was £35 richer in 1877. Perigo managed the treacle store. A lad who grew up in Sydney in the 1870s long after remembered the treacle cart,

---

31 ANU/NBAC, CSR, 142/3563, Colonial Sugar Company Wages Book, 1883–84.

A hearse-like thing with four wheels, a high seat for the driver, and a big tap at the back, from which thick black molasses was run into jugs or basins at sixpence for enough to do a family of ten for quite a week.[32]

Poolman, whom we met in 1854, working overtime on the completion of the refitting of the refinery, and giving evidence to the Health Board in 1875, was now on £600 per annum, and not included in the handout. By now he was in charge of the building of the new refinery at Pyrmont.

In quoting workers' pay at so much a day and then converting this to an annual rate in order to calculate their bonuses, it would be easy to imply that work was regular and guaranteed, but this was not so. The processes carried out at the refinery were seasonal and work was very uneven. Wage sheets for 1883, which would not have been unlike from those of earlier decades, show that days actually worked, and therefore paid for, varied enormously from the norm of a six day, sixty hour week. In slack times it might be one or two, in busy times, more. An engineer called Clare, who appeared officially to work the union-approved eight hour day, forty-eight hour week at twelve shillings a day, appears on a different document as being on an hourly rate of one-and-six (that is, twelve shillings a day), but working for seventy-seven hours, while Dickey, a semi-skilled metal worker, ostensibly working a sixty hour week, in fact put in ninety-four hours. At other times the hours fell well below the official number.[33] This unevenness of work was widespread in Sydney in the last decades of the nineteenth century. It was excellent for employers, but not so easy on the men and their families who were tied into this kind of employment pattern.

It is tempting to speculate on the reasons behind Edward Knox's gift of £1,500 to his workers. Was it for loyalty given in the difficult closing years of operations at Chippendale, when the company's public acceptance was at a low ebb? Was it for services rendered when part of the property was destroyed by fire just before the move to Pyrmont?[34]

Nearby, Tooths brewery continued to grow, though slowly. The second generation of Tooths were taking over the business, and the product was becoming acceptable in colonial society, if the following advertisement which appeared in the *Herald* in 1851 is any guide:

Grand Civic Feast—Required on 1st proximo on which date the Right Worshipful the Mayor retires from office; 30 ham sandwiches, 30 ox tongue sandwiches, with 30 pints of best Cape (decanted) and 30 pints in pewter of Tooths Single X, for the use of the Mayor, Aldermen, and Councillors of the body incorporate.[35]

The brewery remained a fairly small concern during the decades before 1880, with several competitors holding a good share of the market. Some tentative expansion was evident, however in the acquisition of property in Chippendale: six to eight shops and

---

32 *SMH*, 4 July 1933.
33 NBAC, CSR, 142/3563, Colonial Sugar Company, Wages Book 1883–84.
34 NSCA/CRS 17/7/14.
35 Quoted in Tooth and Co Ltd, *The First Hundred Years: A Brief History of Kent Brewery* (1935), p 22.

houses on Parramatta Street and Kensington Street; plus, by 1880, considerable vacant land in Balfour Street.

The most significant newcomer to the area, as employer, was the Redfern Railway Station, which was to be the terminal station for Sydney for over half a century. It was located just outside Chippendale, the smells, noise and black soot of locomotives were constantly visited upon the northern end of the area. Until 1886, when the Eveleigh workshops opened, this was the site of much of the work of the railways. The first government-made locomotive was produced in 1870, although until the eighties most construction was contracted out to private firms, such as Hudson Brothers in Redfern, which built carriages. In general, this new form of transport provided work for the people living nearby. In 1879 the Council assessors produced an inventory of railway property at the terminus, because the Council was arguing that the Government ought to pay rates. Government property never was rated but the 1879 assessment leaves us with a good description of the railway. Apart from the passenger station, the only buildings which were not of wooden construction were the locomotive engine house made of brick with a slate roof, a couple of offices, and workshops for carpenters, trimmers and patternmakers. Most buildings had iron roofs—painters' and plumbers' shops, carriage paint shop, storage and receiving sheds, blacksmithy, boiler sheds and so on. By 1880 the twenty-seven acre site was extremely congested, so that by the early eighties it was necessary to extend the Darling Harbour goods lines to take more country produce and to purchase the Eveleigh Estate for new workshops. As well as the passenger terminal, there was the Mortuary Station in Regent Street, a wondrous Gothic church-like structure from which funeral trains

Chippendale from the railway yards, c. 1870. In the foreground the workshops *(left)* and station *(right)*. In the background *(left to right)*, St Paul's, Cleveland Street tunnel, Wesley Chapel, the Mortuary Station, a grand house on Regent Street, the brewery chimney and tower.

took parties of mourners to the cemetery at Rookwood. The presence of this building provided a stimulus for quite different forms of employment, such as Primrose and Company's funeral parlour in Regent Street and Mrs Dart's florist shop at 12 George Street West.

With the progressive settlement of Chippendale came the churches and their schools. Aside from St Benedict's, an early landmark in the district, the only other church actually within its boundaries was the Wesleyan Chapel, opened in 1847, on Botany Road (Regent Street).[36] Before this, there had briefly been a small chapel in Queen Street. This church became the parent church in the second circuit in Sydney, and, as the city's population grew, the congregation was involved in setting up other chapels in more outlying areas like Pyrmont and Waterloo. An additional land grant in Regent Street in 1865 allowed the chapel to be enlarged to a seating capacity of 800 adults and 500 children. Mrs George Wigram Allen laid the foundation stone on 1 January 1866 at four o'clock and, as was the custom of the day, Mr George Wigram Allen expressed his wife's gratification at being asked to do so. Then they all had tea and a meeting. Replicated with variations by other churches, social activities such as church teas, socials, Sunday School picnics, ladies auxiliaries, jumble sales and Mutual Improvement Societies, where young men and lads heard lectures and learnt to debate and exchange ideas, were not merely avenues for religious expression, but were the mainstay of respectable entertainment and social life in Chippendale. The peak membership at this church was reached in 1873, with '432 members and 64 on trial', but time and again organised activities attracted far greater numbers. When King George of Tonga, a recent convert to Methodism, addressed a meeting in Chippendale in 1853, 'the gathering became more of a camp meeting than what was expected, and extended away over the adjoining paddocks.'[37]

The Anglican St Barnabas, on Parramatta Street, and St Paul's, next to the railway and almost opposite Wesley, both just outside Chippendale's borders, provided similar entertainment along with the services and Bible studies. There was also a substantial amount of practical charity in the form of food and clothing and help in getting work for the poor who lived in the area. Many residents patronised the lot.

All of these churches had schools attached to them, although before 1880 schooling was not compulsory, and no doubt many resisted it, as children were of greater economic benefit doing other things. St Benedict's, long an important school in the Catholic scheme of things, became the training school for Catholic teachers in 1862.[38] There still existed in this period some schools run by private individuals, but this form of education was clearly on the wane.

The other public building which would have affected the lives of Chippendale's poor, if not the better off, was the branch dispensary of the Sydney Hospital which was established in 1871 in Regent Street, in a house owned by Stephen Goold, one of Chippendale's better-known citizens of these years. A painter and glazier by trade, and a lay preacher in

---

36 G.J. Pitt, 'Wesley Church, Chippendale', *Journal of Australasian Methodist Historical Society*, Vol 11, Pt 4, No 7, July 1934, pp 107–15.

37 Ibid, p 108.

38 J.J. Fletcher, *Blackfriars Public School*, NSW Education Department School History files, 1982, p 2.

Mortuary Station, c.1875.

his spare time, he became a political organiser for the Protestant Political Association, which had as its main aim the election of practising Protestant members to political positions. He himself represented Phillip Ward, which included Chippendale, on the City Council 1870–76, and in 1874 was Mayor of Sydney.[39] While he was on the Council, Kensington Lane, later known as Fitzroy Street, was renamed Goold Street, and Charles Street was renamed Balfour. There are various candidates for the naming of this street, but perhaps it was Stephen Goold's gift to his wife Margery, whose family name was Balfour.

It was not public buildings which interested some people so much as public houses. There was one almost on every corner, it seemed. With so many small cottages and tenements there was very little room to relax or entertain 'at home'—that was a bourgeois pretension unheard of in most Chippendale households. Entertainment was usually home grown, but took place in the pubs or the street. Hours of selling liquor were unrestricted and public places of drinking included many doorsteps. The streets and paddocks provided space for cricket and fights, of the organised, pugilist variety, and of the more spontaneous sort, and often involving both sexes.

The less violent sport of fishing was no longer carried out in Chippendale, but the waterhole across the road on the corner of the University (now officially designated a 'lake') offered possibilities. This was for many years a popular place for washing down

39 Mark Lyons, 'Goold, Stephen Styles (1817–1876)' *ADB*, Vol. 4, 1966, p 267.

Wesley Schoolhouse and Chapel, Regent Street c.1870.

horses and vehicles before the last haul into town. Otherwise, the would-be angler walked to Pyrmont or Darling Harbour. Increasingly, care had to be taken in choosing a spot at a distance from the discharge of the city's sewers, although the blood and offal washed into the waters from the Glebe Island Abattoirs, unpleasant as it was to most, can only have increased the fisherman's chances of success.

Aside from such self-generated recreations, there was not much on offer. The theatres in town were not exclusive, but they did require money. So did the racecourses. Many people went only where they could walk, and Homebush (which operated until 1860) and Randwick were both at a distance. With time, train and omnibus fares became more accessible, but not for many and usually not for children. The occasional crowd entertainments, such as air balloon ascents and organised processions, usually occurred at the Domain end of town, at least until 1869 when the first Royal Agricultural Show was held in new buildings in Prince Alfred Park, newly created from the Cleveland Paddocks. It was the presence of the railway terminal which made this park a popular entertainment venue, and it became the centre for circuses, animal shows and celebrations such as the Scottish Highland games.

Those who chose not to spend their pennies on such things could, towards the close of the 1870s, hand them over to William O'Neill, the postmaster on George Street West, for safekeeping in the Government Savings Bank. Larger depositors could patronise the Bank of New Wales, which opened in 1860 at the corner of Parramatta Street and Regent Street. This was the Bank's first city branch and again it was the railway which made this the favoured location for expansion. Here the Bank's smelting works formed much of the colony's gold into ingots, so that in keeping with Chippendale's increasing industrialisation, this was a bank which belched smoke from its coke-fired furnaces, located in Regent Street behind the commercial building.[40]

In the first chapter we saw how Chippendale became the location for much substandard housing in the 1840s. For the period of this chapter, we have several detailed housing studies to draw on, including that of W.S. Jevons. In the fifties Jevons, who later became a noted British economist, worked as an assayer in the Mint in Sydney. While in the colonies, he began to develop an interest in what he called 'the scientific investigation of man', and one of the legacies of this transitional period in his thinking is his *Social Survey of Australian Cities*, published in 1858.[41] In this, prefiguring the work of social geographers of our own time, Jevons attempted to map the land uses of Sydney, so that by showing the distribution of housing, industry and commerce, and the directions of traffic flows, he might analyse 'the whole internal organization or machinery of the city'. He divided housing into three classes corresponding to social position, with the third class representing the poor or labouring people. In his list of 'lowest and least desirable localities', he included the northern section of Chippendale. Of the whole area, he commented that most houses were third class, with a few second class and even one or two first class houses (that is, those belonging to 'all who may be termed gentlemen and ladies') on Botany Road. The main roads contained some small businesses and the occasional hotel, but inside these boundaries, poor housing dominated.

In 1876 the Health Board set up a committee to investigate housing in Sydney, and once again Chippendale came in for some stiff criticism. Poor drainage, resulting in local flooding and accumulations of stagnant foul sewage, was referred to frequently. But because the process of housing is dynamic, the committee did not always isolate the same places for criticism. Kensington Street, for example, which was so unacceptable to Jevons, they considered to be satisfactory—'houses were in good order . . . the yards clean, the drains connected with a sewer, and the closets fitted with patent cisterns.' Paradise Row, on the other hand, had not improved any. Some of these cottages were empty 'on account probably of their uninhabitable condition', and in general these houses were 'in a filthy condition and in very bad repair'. However, their inspection was fairly cursory, because many of the tenants, urged on by the agent, refused them entry. This, they said, was the first time that anyone had offered any resistance to their inspection.[42] It would not be the last time that Chippendale residents resisted the intrusions of landlords, government officials and municipal officers to their premises for the purposes of study, eviction and the like.

At the end of Paradise Row stood an old brick and slate four-roomed house, formerly sound enough, but by 1876, 'in such a tottering state that it is a matter of surprise that people should be found so venturesome as to live in it'. One of these rooms was used by Mr Hodgkinson, of the Sydney City Mission. Founded in 1862, this organisation was

---

40 J. J. Paris, 'The Southern Gate of Sydney Town', in *The Etruscan* (house journal of Bank of NSW) Sept 1960, pp 30–31; the editor, *The Etruscan*, July 1978, pp 2–3.

41 W. S. Jevons, 'Social Survey of Australian Cities, 1858' (ML, MS B864).

42 SCSSHB, *Eleventh Progress Report*, NSW V&P, LA, 1875–6, Vol 5, p 611.

Clockwise from top: Holtermann's Hotel, corner of Abercrombie Place and Cooper Street, c. 1875. The publican was Timothy Hart. This fine terrace was part of the replacement of Cooper's Rookery; Emu Inn, corner of Outram and Regent streets; The Old Duke of Wellington, corner of Greeves Lane and George Street West, c. 1885; James Leonard's Royal Oak, corner of Abercrombie Place and Wattle Street, c. 1875. A hotel of this name, but of different construction, is still there.

inspired by the London City Mission and was intended to be a non-denominational force for Christianity sending missionaries into the darkest parts of the city where regular church activities would not penetrate. Paradise Row then took on a different meaning. In 1876 the commissioners observed that 'this worthy man' had done much good in 'this disreputable locality', but Canon Stephen, rector of nearby St Paul's, complained that he poached several of his 'well-to-do people', who thereby gave donations to the Mission which the good Canon believed were due to him. An investigation by the Mission found that 'Mr Hodgkinson had not encouraged respectable people to come to his meeting'.[43]

Social divisions in the 1870s were not likely to entice many of the well-heeled into Paradise Row. Incidentally, it is interesting that although this lane had officially been called Smithers Street as early as 1858, 'Paradise Row' stuck to it for many years. The city assessors, who sometimes annotated their books with standardised comments like 'not fit for occupation', were moved to record of this street in 1867 the heartfelt remark 'miserable place'. The Health Board Commissioners completed their 1876 report on Paradise Row by observing that they could not imagine that the owner actually knew how bad the places were, otherwise he would have had them pulled down and decent tenements built.

The significance and intent of this observation would not have been missed by contemporary readers of the report. The row was owned by Thomas Broughton, and had been for at least thirty years. Its notoriety made it most unlikely that he did not know. Broughton owned vast tracts of urban housing, had been a member of the city council, and was elected Mayor in 1846. He was one of those men who had pulled himself up by the bootstraps, and had no sympathy for his fellow citizens who were less fortunate or more profligate.[44]

Until the end of the 1870s, the Council had no power to order demolition of buildings, but they sometimes achieved it through moral persuasion, helped along by prosecutions for creating a nuisance. Linden Lane, for instance, singled out in 1859 as the poorest in the area, had been pulled down in response to municipal pressure by 1876 or possibly through a realisation that the time was ripe for using the land more profitably.

By the 1860s the last large land holdings in Chippendale had been subdivided. The Kensington Estate, next to the brewery, had seen some occupation, mostly in Kensington Street itself, in the forties, but after the coming of the railway in 1855 this area began to fill with houses in a series of narrow little streets which have since been reorganised. One of the last areas to be subdivided was Hutchinson's paddock, an extensive watercress bed which joined Shepherd's Nursery. Most of it was in Redfern, but it extended into Chippendale, and with its subdivision, Cleveland Street, was surveyed through to Newtown Road. Thus, although this eventually became an important through road, it was not so at this stage. In 1858, in its first year of publication, *Sands Directory* listed only eight houses between Newtown Road and St Paul's church and school on the corner of Botany Street (now Regent). By 1865 there were a dozen houses and one public house, and by 1880, although the first few rows of terrace housing had appeared and the hotels numbered four, there were still many free-standing cottages and several stretches of vacant land along the road.

---

43 June Owen, *The Heart of the City: The First 125 Years of the Sydney City Mission* (1987), p 24.
44 Helen Bowd, 'Broughton, Thomas Stafford (1810–1901)', *ADB*, Vol 3, 1966, pp 253–54.

This picture dates from about 1900. The wall appears to have an interesting bow.

On the other hand, Parramatta Street, recently renamed George Street West in recognition that the city did indeed include Chippendale, was built out and beginning to experience its second wave of construction. Shops and manufacturing establishments outnumbered houses, and many were still run down. Produce stores, a boot factory and a pawn shop represented Chippendale's old ways, but there were new signs of commercial strengthening: a post office, and a seventeen-roomed English and Scottish Chartered Bank in 'Fowlers Corner' building at the Newtown Road end; a three storey, twenty-five room Southern Railway Hotel at the railway end. There were still some wooden shacks, and tiny one-up, one-down terraces, but they were gradually being replaced by three storey brick and slate house/shop combination buildings.

Not all of Chippendale was 'improving'. On Regent Street, for instance, what previously had been mostly residential was becoming more industrial, no doubt due to the railway's proximity. There was a coach factory, timber yard, hay store, Hume and Pegrum's lemonade factory, an undertaker and so on. The large mansions of earlier times were being downgraded. At Number 25, for example, Mrs Alice Slattery ran a private school, while next door Mrs Pike ran a boarding house.

But if the fortunes of individual streets rose and fell, the overall status of Chippendale did not change much. Settlement went on apace with very little restraint and increasing problems. As in the rest of Sydney, rapid development was occurring 'on the run' as it were, with considerable confusion being generated about who was responsible for what. When Sir Daniel Cooper was rated for property on Cleveland Street, he agreed to pay for some of it, but not all because he said some of the lots of land did not exist. The Council's officers were fairly sure that they did, but in the end the City Treasurer had to admit that from 'the lack of any map or plans, they are all completely beyond the power of identification . . . the Council are helpless in this matter'. [45] On the other hand, confusion could be deliberately fostered.

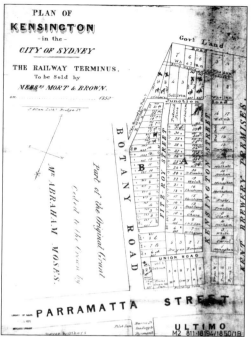

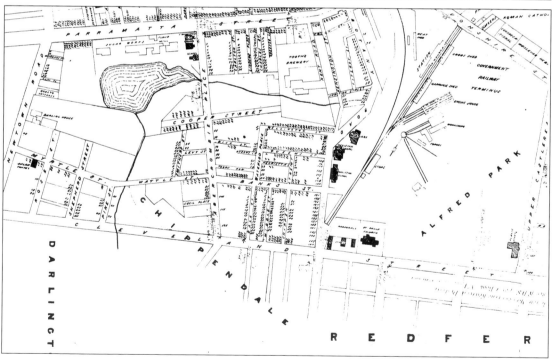

Top: Kensington . . . at the Railway Terminus, 1850. The creek at the end of Kensington Street caused access problems for many years to come. *Above:* Section of Hunt and Stevens map, 1868. Chippendale is still far from being built out.

George Street West, c. 1885.

In the mid-1870s, at about the time the Council was unable to control the CSR's discharge of foul water into Blackwattle Swamp, some powerful private citizens of The Glebe had managed to get the courts to order the Council to refrain from making any further connections to the sewer. So when the Harbour and Rivers Department asked if they could connect an additional pipe to this sewer, to carry sewage from The Glebe, the City Engineer advised that this would overload an already malfunctioning system and would be a disaster. Then, in the same memorandum, as an afterthought, he added 'if by granting, this would relieve the Corporation from the Injunction then it should be sanctioned at once'.[46] So much for sound engineering or community protection.

Considerable environmental problems were piling up in Chippendale in this period of post-gold rush expansion, but it was during its next phase of development that the area was to become most notorious for these problems.

---

45 NSCA CRS 26/178/1481, 24 August 1881.
46 NSCA CRS 26/116/675; 26/153/908.

3

FROM 1880 TO 1914

THE DECADE STRADDLING 1880 was one of explosive growth in Sydney. It was in these years that much of the terrace housing which we currently associate with Victorian Sydney was erected, and, as we have seen, in the case of an inner area such as Chippendale this was often second generation housing. As land in the city centre was increasingly used for offices and shops, locations further out, like Chippendale, became more valued for residential and manufacturing purposes. Chippendale was never completely residential, but in so far as it had a residential phase, it was in the three decades after 1880. Between 1871 and 1891, while inner city wards lost population, Chippendale (Phillip Ward) increased its numbers by over fifty per cent. This was not as great an increase as in Surry Hills, next door, or in parts of Pyrmont, but a respectable growth rate nonetheless.

In the city, if not the suburbs, drainage and sewage had gradually been extended and made more efficient, but in some areas, including parts of Chippendale, improvement proved elusive and environmental degradation accelerated. The gradual reclamation of the swamp land at the mouth of the Blackwattle Creek was one 'improvement' with mixed blessings. In 1881 the City Engineer had reported that the whole district was gradually being reclaimed, to everyone's satisfaction, but a few years later he had changed his tune. In March 1883 residents in Ultimo, across the road from Chippendale, petitioned the Council because they had 'of late years been visited by divers and grievous inundations'. They argued that the New Wentworth Park which the government had built at the mouth of the creek had formed a dam, so that whenever Sydney had a rainstorm, their houses were flooded, 'submerging their floors, furniture and chattels in several feet of foul noisome stormwater'. They asked for an additional drain. The engineer appended a note to the petition, saying the information was 'very accurate', and recommended that the drain be built. However he was not hopeful of an easy solution. The slope of the land was too slight, the relationship between the two relevant authorities—namely, the Government, which was reclaiming the swamp, and the Council, which provided the sewers—was fraught, and consequently he believed these houses would have to be demolished and the whole of the ground built up.

The flooding on occasions also affected land back in Chippendale and ironically, just as improvements at the mouth led to problems in Ultimo, so improvements in Ultimo led to problems in Chippendale for decades to come. The decision to cover the open sewer in 1900 resulted in back flooding through manholes, gullies, yards and cellars, while the eventual resumption and building up of the worst areas of Ultimo similarly prevented effective drainage in Chippendale.[1] Lawsuits and compensation payments relating to this area occurred for years.

---

1 NSCA CRS 26/183/408; 26/185/982, 110; 26/187/1577; 26/190/489 (petition); NSCA CRS 28/3549/10.

And, in case this were not enough to contend with, an illegal subdivision of the old Sugar Company land on Parramatta Street became the subject of public outcry and debate in the 1880s. Once again Chippendale was on the map as an environmental disaster area.

The land was sold to A.H. McCulloch, C.F. Stokes and R.S. Black in 1878, for £47,500, 'being £2,500 more than the amount at which it was valued in the previous Half-Years

Henry Gorman, real estate agent.

Richard Seymour, City Nuisance Inspector.

accounts'. Urban land prices were rising, and the prospect of so much residential land so close to the city centre augured well for Andrew McCulloch, who was the active party in this subdivision. A solicitor involved in land conveyancing who eventually became a land dealer on a large scale, McCulloch had become a member of parliament in the previous year (1877), at the age of 34. He was a personal friend of John Lackey, land jobber and Minister for Public Works in the Parkes-Robertson ministry of 1878, was director of several building societies and closely tied to the land auctioneers, Hardie and Gorman. Henry Gorman was a friend of Sir Henry Parkes.[2]

McCulloch had the land subdivided into town allotments, having demolished the refinery buildings, 'which for so many years have been an eyesore'.[3] The stone was auctioned off, with preference being given to purchasers of the land, so perhaps some of Chippendale's past was recycled in the new houses which were built over the next few years on the eleven and a half acre subdivision called the Blackfriars Estate, inspired by the presence of St Benedict's church and school next door to the property. If the presale advertisements of Hardie and Gorman could be believed, it was 'the most important and valuable city freehold that had been submitted to public competition at any one time in the City of Sydney', and the layout of the land, allegedly chosen from 'about thirty competitive plans', would please the prospective buyer. The estate commanded 'a very noble frontage . . . to George Street West', and the plans advertising the sale of the subdivision included an artist's impression of 'George Street West as it should be', featuring fine modern business houses.[4]

But the advertising hype went further. 1879 was a big year in Sydney's social calender, as the city was host to the first International Exhibition ever held in Australia, in the new

2 NBAC.CSR, Z303, 4.1.0., Document 2, Board Minutes, 10 February 1879. For an interesting discussion on McCulloch and friends, see Lesley Muir, 'Public Spending and Private Property: The Illawarra Line Cabal' in Max Kelly (ed), *Sydney City of Suburbs* (1987), pp 36–42.

3 *SMH*, 22 January 1879.

4 A reproduction of this advertisement is displayed in the boardroom of Hardie and Gorman, Baillieu Group, Sydney. Also ML.

The estate agent's grand vision for George Street West.

and spectacular Garden Palace built in the Botanical Gardens for the event. The purveyors of Blackfriars announced that 'a mammoth hotel on the American principle, capable of comfortably accommodating 10,000 to 15,000 persons' could suitably be built on the site which was alleged to be close to everything of consequence in the city, despite the fact that Chippendale was at the opposite end of the city from The Domain where the Exhibition was to be held. 'Citizens desiring to take part in this truly national undertaking' were invited to attend the sale of the Blackfriars Estate. [5] But no such hotel was built, and there was no stampede to buy the land of the old Sugar Company. The blocks sold slowly, and a year and a half later in September 1881, Hardie and Gorman readvertised the Blackfriars Estate, but this time, with a little over one third of the blocks still unsold, the flamboyance had gone out of their sales pitch. With no fuss, they simply advertised an 'absolute sale, to clear . . . the cheapest city building land'. Similarly when Shepherd's Nursery adjoining the Blackfriars Estate was subdivided in 1883, the agents, Richardson and Wrench, did not vaunt the wonders of the place. In fact, as if to reassure people that the land was worth buying at all, they announced that it 'was solid from old, and . . . the best of foundations for any size and weight structure that can be built'. [6]

Behind the varying rhetoric of these advertisements there had evolved a tale of woe for sellers and purchasers alike. It is a story of greed and deception, as well as of incompetence and administrative bungling. Its retelling will help to illuminate the tensions which existed in this late nineteenth century city between private developers and the municipal government on the one hand, and, more importantly, between the Sydney Corporation and the colonial government, on the other. The reader may judge whether the real losers in this affair were any of the above, or whether they were the ordinary people who lived in Chippendale.

At a superficial level, problems arose from the difficulty of making well watered industrial land into well-drained residential land. McCulloch was aware of potential drainage problems, and at the time the subdivision was made he requested that the City Corporation form a street which he proposed to build to facilitate the movement of storm water. The old dam had been drained, but the original watercourse could cause flooding in heavy rain. Without much sensitivity McCulloch called this Stream Street, soon changed to Buckland Street. Even today, after many alterations to the road levels, it is still apparent that Buckland Street follows roughly the course of the old Blackwattle Swamp Creek. As we have seen, the City Council had been saying for years that such drainage had to be dealt with, and its surveyor was of the opinion that McCulloch's proposals were sound, yet they were not acted on. Council officers continued to recommend improvements to the Blackfriars Estate in the following years. A.C. Mountain, City Surveyor, recommended improvements in 1880, as did Richard Seymour, the Nuisance Inspector, who:

> found the stagnant pool, about which so much correspondence has lately taken place, in a most filthy state, the water being perfectly black and the stench arising from it perfectly intolerable. There is scarcely a house in the vicinity and not one in the

5 SMH, 22 January 1879.
6 SMH, 19 August 1881; 14 July 1883.

immediate locality which is free from typhoid or gastric fever or some other disease
caused doubtless by the exhalation from the pestiferous pool?[7]

He recommended diverting drainage into the Abercrombie Street sewer, as had been suggested several years previously to deal with the Sugar Company's dam.

But none of these things was done, for what the officers recommended on rational grounds the Council rejected for political reasons. The roads of the Blackfriars Estate were left unmade for many years because the area was singled out by the Council as a scapegoat in its battle to achieve compliance with its rules and regulations covering subdivisions.

At the time that the estate was being subdivided, legislation was being drawn up for a new Corporation Act, which was passed in July 1879. This act, and also the City of Sydney Improvement Act passed the same year, made it illegal to create roads of less width than sixty-six feet and lanes of less than twenty feet. In 1881 this was made more general for the colony, in the Width of Streets and Lanes Act, commonly known as Reid's Act.[8] All of this legislation was passed *after* the subdivision of the Blackfriars Estate, but *before* the streets had been made, thus rendering their making illegal. If the Council had wanted to assist the subdivider rather than holding to the letter of the law, they would probably have been able to do so without much public interest being aroused, but the Council did not wish to. Instead, it chose to use this subdivision as a testing ground for its strength, in an attempt to bring a wayward real estate industry into line. From the distance of today it is difficult to determine just why the Council chose to make an example of this subdivision. Illegal subdivisions were everyday affairs in Sydney, and not confined to any particular firms or individuals. Possibly animosity was aroused by the knowledge that members of parliament were involved, who were legislating for one thing, while doing another. Possibly there was enough residual bad feeling about the Sugar Company's land to make this the chosen test case. Possibly it was selected because of recent quarrels with Hardie and Gorman. The year before the Blackfriars subdivision, this firm had subdivided and sold thirty-one allotments of Chippendale land for Thomas Broughton, and at that time had asked the Council to kerb and gutter streets of only thirty feet. The Council's City Surveyor was instructed to tell Hardie and Gorman that under the legislation (old legislation, preceding 1879) no street was to be less than forty feet. And now, a year later Hardie and Gorman were at it again, with the widths of some of the streets on the Blackfriars Estate not even complying with the more lax pre-1879 Corporation Act, let alone the current legislation. The Council dug its heels in, and the people who bought land on the estate got no made roads, gutters or drains. With streets unformed and drainage defects all too plain to see, the land did not sell rapidly. When Hardie and Gorman notified the Council of the second sale in June 1881, they again asked the Council to form the streets, this time offering to pay some of the costs. There was a certain amount of disbelief that the Council would stand firm. After all, it did not have a history of interfering with the real estate fraternity.

---

7 NSCA/CRS 26/156/368; the majority of the correspondence relating to Blackfriars is at NSCA/CRS 30/1/67—
Blackfriars Estate—Correspondence ordered to be printed, 30 August 1883.
8 NSCA/CRS 26/145/571, Hardie and Gorman to T. C., 7 June 1877.

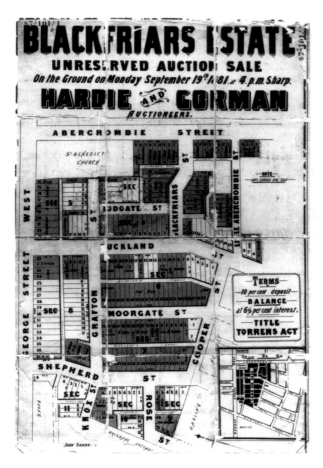

Andrew McCulloch, politician and land dealer.

The sales pitch is more restrained. The roads are the same width as before.

But the Council did stand firm. The subdividers were politely informed that no approval had ever been given for the subdivision, and that the Council declined all responsibility for it. Hardie and Gorman, ignoring all this, held their second sale of land on the Blackfriars Estate in September 1881. Perhaps the agents suffered reduced sale prices, but in fact no direct action could be taken against them as none of the legislation provided for any penalties for illegal subdivisions.

In the years following these sales, buildings went up. McCulloch himself built a number of shops on the corner of George Street West and Buckland Street which obstructed the culvert under George Street West, in what must have been a deliberate attempt to force the Council to act.[9] Needless to say McCulloch was not personally inconvenienced. In 1882 he bought 'Weemalla', a house in the mountains at Faulconbridge, where the air was pure.[10]

Angry correspondence and petitions piled up in the Town Clerk's office. In 1883, 115 residents wrote complaining that Buckland Street not only received too much drainage,

---

9 NSCA/CRS 30/1/67, City Surveyor to Mayor, 25 June 1880.
10 Alfred Stephen, 'Numantia', *JRAHS*, Vol XXXI, Pt IV, 1945, pp 264, 275.

but was used by 'sundry persons' to deposit garbage and night soil, dead animals and broken glass—mounds of it, which was forming into an embankment at the end of the street. This area was 'a slough' which was not only stinking and a danger to health, but was according to the petitioners, becoming a location for 'immoral and illegal practices'. It is difficult to know why this might have been, except that cleanliness and godliness often routinely went together in the Victorian mind, and so, presumably, did their opposites. The Council did nothing. Indeed, a letter from Nicholas Conroy of the Victoria Hotel on the corner of Buckland Street, complaining of this same 'embankment' was annotated by the surveyor: 'The "street" in question is on the Blackfriars Estate; all these streets and lanes the Council has declined in anyway to acknowledge.'[11]

In addition to problems caused by the Blackfriars subdivision, the construction of a tramway along George Street West had created another set of difficulties. This required that the level of the road be raised in the vicinity of the creek. Builders on Blackfriars Estate, being advised that this would happen, built high up and then threatened to sue the Council for compensation when the level was not altered soon enough. When the alterations were made in 1882, heavy rain destroyed part of the main culvert at one stage, causing the flooding of buildings on the north side of the road. The construction of a retaining wall ultimately left buildings on the other side of the road, in Ultimo, partially

10–20 Irving Street, c. 1910.

11 NSCA CRS 26/189/290; 26/190/392.

obscured. The Council was prepared to compensate in these cases, but not for flooding. When Mrs Walsh, a widow with 'five helpless children', had her shop cellar flooded out because a sewer was interfered with while the tramline was built, she asked for compensation. It was denied because the sewer was an illegal one—one of the many constructed by desperate residents who lived in this area. [12] Even despite the altered street levels, this part of George Street West still flooded in times of heavy rain, sometimes stopping trams altogether.

Then, in 1883, presumably in an attempt to support their business brothers and render the acts impotent, the land adjoining Blackfriars, previously Shepherd's Nursery, was subdivided by Richardson and Wrench for the Haymarket Permanent Land Building and Investment Company Limited. Again, in contravention of the law, the streets were a mere 50 feet and the lanes only twelve to fourteen feet. Council sent its Town Clerk to the auction sale to read a statement explaining the legalities of the situation to prospective buyers. [13]

By now however tempers were frayed in Chippendale, and certain aldermen, no doubt with an eye on the next election, began to urge that action be taken in the name of public health. Despite the fact that legal opinion had reassured the Council that they were in the right, following the sale of the Shepherd's Nursery Estate there was a move within Council to take over these streets in 1884. However, Council's legal advice was that not only could they refuse to make the roads, but that regardless of Council resolutions, they could not ever make them, without breaking the law.

In the meantime, the mire that was developing in Chippendale was exacerbated by the decision of the government to build a public school on the Blackfriars Estate. Here we will digress a little to fill in the background to this decision, as it put Chippendale's children right in the forefront of a bitter battle which had been raging in New South Wales for a number of years, concerning the appropriate role of the state and the church in educating the colony's youth.

Prior to 1880, as we have seen, if the children of Chippendale went to school at all, they had a choice of government schools or church schools or even a few lingering privately run schools. Since the 1866 Public Schools Act, a Council of Education had run the government schools and contributed to the cost of church schools which complied with certain requirements on buildings and curricula. During the 1870s agitation grew for the withdrawal of state aid from church schools. Sectarian bitterness ran deep, and harsh words were widely flung. In 1880 the Public Instruction Act was passed, including provision for all assistance to church schools to cease by the end of 1882. It also ruled that education would be compulsory. Both these provisions meant that the new Department of Education set up by the Act was to embark on an immediate building program in anticipation of huge increases in numbers of children in the state schools. In fact, in 1880 an extra 20,000 did turn up across New South Wales. [14]

---

12 NSCA/CRS 26/185//1006.

13 *NSWPD*, LA 1889, Vol XL, p 3494.

14 J. Fletcher and J. Burnswood, *Government Schools of New South Wales since 1848* (1988), pp 9–11.

Blackfriars Public School, built 1885.

In 1881 the Department resumed land in Chippendale, partly from St Benedict's, mostly from McCulloch. There are letters on their files from Hardie and Gorman urging the resumption, and a note from the Department's Under-Secretary stating that the Minister for Education, John Robertson, was 'desirous that this case should be treated as a very urgent one'. McCulloch, whose land was not selling well, was anxious to oblige the Department, while St Benedict's was unhappy about their land being reduced, especially when in 1883 a further small resumption which encroached on the newly built Presbytery stables and laundry was found to be necessary. In November 1881 the government school inspector recommended building a school to hold 1,500 pupils—possibly the largest school building project undertaken at any one time in the nineteenth century. [15]

The choice of this site, in the middle of a bog, and hard by the Catholic school, is difficult to explain on rational grounds. Similarly, the decision to build to accommodate such a large number of children is puzzling. In November 1881 when this recommendation was made there were about 700 children in daily attendance at St Benedict's and St Barnabas School on George Street West combined. It was expected that after the 1880 Education Act, most of the Anglican Schools would close, but given the importance Roman Catholics placed on religious education, and their tendency to equate state

15 SRNSW:NRS 3829, [5/14945] and NRS 3828, [6/66]—Index—New Schools 1880–2 (Blackfriars is filed under Parramatta Street). Also J. J. Fletcher, *Blackfriars Public School* (1982).

St Benedict's School, Abercrombie Street.

education with the works of the devil, it was unlikely that all of their schools would shut, least of all a school like St Benedict's, attached to an important Catholic church in a strongly Catholic area. Nevertheless, the provision for 1,500 pupils suggests that possibly closure of St Benedict's was hoped for by Department of Education planners. But there were many in the 1880s who believed that rather than being motivated by this perhaps naive hope, the construction of Blackfriars school was a deliberate act of sectarian bigotry. This interpretation could only have been helped by the choice of G.A. Mansfield to design the buildings, because the Department's architect, Kemp, was too busy to deal with it. Had Kemp designed it, the school would have been squarer, more Classical. Mansfield, who had designed schools in the sixties and seventies, favoured the Gothic, religious style. [16] And so, cheek by jowl with the simple church school there arose a grand church-like state school. It generated a lot of anger.

Cardinal Moran, Archbishop of Sydney.

The Catholic Archbishop, Moran, recently arrived in the colony, visited the St Benedict's School in September 1884 and was reported in the press as telling the children that he was 'pained and grieved to see other schools encroaching on your ground'. He alleged that the public school cut off light from the church school and summarised the construction of the school as

> *The cruelest act of intolerance . . . an act of unfairness and injustice and vandalism. The State has boundless resources at hand—its grounds not limited—yet it casts its eyes on your little home of religion and science. (Applause) The lesson you should learn from this is have nothing to do with such Public Schools.* [17]

A difficult lesson, under the circumstances.

Official inquiries followed this outburst, which informed the Minister for Education, now W.J. Trickett, that the building did block the sun, but only a little bit and only in the afternoons. Possibly Trickett was less concerned about this than he was to support the rightness of the school due to his business connections. He was a director of several land investment companies which also had Henry Gorman on their boards, and shared directorships with F.A. Wright, MP, who was a business associate of Andrew McCulloch. [18]

The resumptions of land 'situated in Blackwattle Swamp', as the Education Department's solicitors put it, were completed in early 1884, and the buildings in April 1885. The school had been operating in the old St Barnabas school buildings and was in

---

16 Ibid.

17 *Daily Telegraph*, 27 September 1884, filed at SRNSW.

18 Trickett and Gorman were both directors of the Anglo–Australian Investment Finance and Land Company and of the NSW Trustees Executors and Agency Company. Wright was director of the latter and of the National Permanent Building, Land and Investment Company of which McCulloch was trustee.

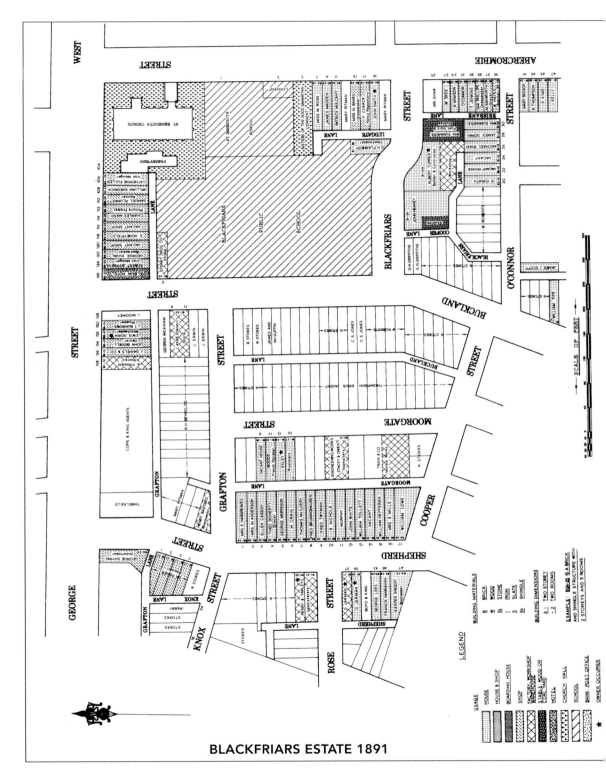

BLACKFRIARS ESTATE 1891

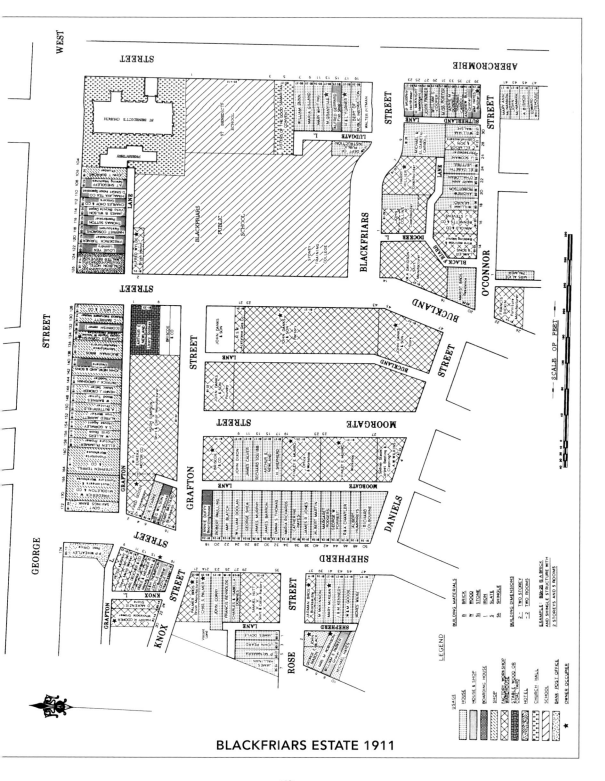

BLACKFRIARS ESTATE 1911

fact the St Barnabas School, but since the end of 1882, funded by the state. The headmaster, John W. Turner, moved the children into the new buildings at the end of April. Two weeks later he managed to find time to write to the Education Department asking for the fifteen shillings he was out of pocket from paying the carrier who moved the school's effects across the road.[19] By the end of May, 792 pupils were enrolled at the school, though attendances would have been well down on that, because the new Act made it compulsory for children to attend only for 'seventy days in each half year', or three days a week, and many children and their parents believed that was quite enough.

Now the Education Department as well as the City Council began receiving petitions praying that the area be cleaned up, drained and maintained. But if the subdividers had hoped that the presence of this grand school would move the Council to make the roads, they were disappointed, until 1886.

It is unclear just why the Council decided to act, but it may have been the psychological impact of these children which tipped the balance. In any case questions were asked about the state of the school in the parliament and in October 1886 a bill was introduced on behalf of the Council, to allow it to take over the roads. The bill, of one clause, passed the lower house without debate, and there is no need to question which way McCulloch and his business associates voted. However, the upper house was unwilling to pass it, with a majority of speakers using arguments similar to those previously used by the Council. The subdivision was illegal, and to sanction it would be to undermine the Corporation Act and give all real estate developers a field day. If the bill were passed, said Sir Alfred Stephen, it would 'enable the proprietors of this estate to put more money into their pockets than by law . . . they should be allowed to do'. It seemed to one member, Thornton, an ex-Mayor of the City, that it would simply 'make bad worse' and that if it were passed it should be called 'An act to perpetuate the evil and the abomination of the Blackfriars Estate within the City of Sydney'. There was even a suggestion that the houses should be pulled down and the purchasers compensated. In the end it was referred to a select committee, which did not report.[20]

All this procrastination produced one unexpected good result. Faced with this apparently intractable problem, state and church temporarily suspended their differences in 1887, when both contributed £7.10.0 to build an illegal sewer through the laneway between the church and the Blackfriars School.[21]

Finally, in September 1889, ten years after the first subdivision, an act was passed allowing the Council to take over the streets and lanes on the Blackfriars and Shepherd's Nursery Estates. There is little doubt that if the Council had made the streets without benefit of legal sanction no one would have demurred, so in this sense, the act did not 'allow', but 'forced' the Council to act. The debates over the bill were long and confused, with blame for the situation attributed to various quarters. According to some, its passage

---

19 SRNSW: NRS 3829, [5/14945].
20 *NSWPD*, LC 1885–6, Vol XXIII, pp 5845–49.
21 SRNSW: NRS 3829, [5/14945].

would be setting a precedent for future illegal subdivisions, and while one member alleged that no other illegal subdivisions had occurred since Reid's Act was passed in 1887, another claimed that Reid's Act was 'not worth a farthing . . . it has been violated with impunity'. As a real estate agent and as a suburban mayor, this member seemed quite happy to admit complicity in many illegal transactions. Some thought the developers ought to be punished, but others believed that they had been punished enough in having investments tied up for so many years. In any case McCulloch, no longer the Member for Cumberland, had been declared bankrupt in October 1888. The particular contribution of the Blackfriars Estate to this state of affairs is uncertain as he had vast land and building dealings all over the colony, but by 1889 there were still thirty-four of the 225 allotments unsold. He died insolvent in 1908.[22] Some believed the Council had been the only honourable party, whilst others thought it could have done more, legally, to restrain Hardie and Gorman, and Richardson and Wrench. It was claimed in parliament that the Council had accepted rates for the housing on the estate, making it 'deserving of the utmost censure', although there is no evidence in the Council's records that they had ever rated this land. The government's role was also dishonourable, it was argued, for resuming land for a school on the site. Some also wondered at the validity of the Land Titles Office accepting the titles of illegally subdivided land.[23]

As an exercise in raising public awareness this whole episode was probably a success, although the claim of one member that there was no 'likelihood of the evil being repeated' and that 'if a subdivision were put before the public now . . . the land [would not] change hands' seemed unduly optimistic. In the end the questions of principle were left unresolved and the bill passed out of sheer embarrassment on the government's part. It claimed the act had been in the interests of public health and for the sake of 'a number of small houses there for the purchase of which poor people have spent their all', although that overstated the case, as most of the poor people on the estate rented, while the owners were not poor at all.

Following the resolution of these legal problems things began to improve materially in the area. But residential development was only partially successful. The maps of land holding (pages 72 and 73) on the Blackfriars Estate have been compiled from information in the Council's Assessment Books and *Sands Directory*. They are representational only, and are no doubt incorrect in some of their finer details, but they do show the changing land uses in this area. The first shows clearly the arrested development of the subdivision in 1891, just after the act of parliament providing for Council services in the area. The thirty-five blocks owned by R. Stokes represent land effectively still unsold, while other purchasers have still not built on their holdings. Only Shepherd Street shows strong residential building. The later map indicated that the trend was towards industrial activities, with a smattering of food processing and clothing workshops, but a preponderance of metal workshops and engineering factories.

---

22 SRNSW: NRS 13654, File No. 22848, [2/10410]. Insolvency File 1887.
23 *NSWPD*, LA 1889, Vol XL, pp 3489–99.

Brewery dray, c. 1910.

The brewery, too, was consolidating. Increased competition in the industry in the 1870s had resulted in intensification to secure the market, with Tooths becoming a public company in 1888. Changes to licensing laws in 1882 had resulted in public houses closing after eleven at night and on Sundays. This meant that bottled beer became more popular and therefore a bottling plant became necessary. As an adjunct to this the company began producing aerated waters in 1883. The factory was extended in 1896, after the little old houses in Greeves Lane were bought up and demolished, and although the actual acreage taken by the brewery had not altered much at this stage, the Company's policy of buying up houses in the streets surrounding the brewery was a portent of things to come. By 1891 it owned houses in Kensington Street, Wellington Street and more extensively than before on George Street West.

By 1896 parts of Balfour Street were being purchased, by 1902, houses in O'Connor Street, and by 1906, Irving Street. As well, the brewery, like other breweries, was from the 1880s buying up hotel properties, and 'tying' publicans to them by advancing them capital in exchange for an agreement to sell their beer. [24]

The people who lived in Chippendale did not, of course, spend all their time worrying about drainage and sewage or property acquisitions. The city became more integrated at this stage of its development, and there was much in it to enjoy. The toll gate had gone and the trams had arrived, steaming first down George Street West and then along Botany Road, now called Regent Street, but advertised boldly at its corner as the road 'to Botany'. At Botany was a picnic ground, a zoo and the chance of a good time for those who had the

---

24 G.J.R. Linge, *Industrial Awakening* (1979), pp 519–24.

fare. As the 1880s progressed, picnic areas further south became accessible by train, and the eastern beaches of Coogee and later Bondi were provided with tram services—although at this time sea bathing was not socially acceptable. The 'picnic' was a widespread custom, announcing in an ostentatious way that its participants were 'at leisure'. Trams were cheap compared with other forms of transport, and greatly enlarged the world for ordinary people.

Closer to home, the Benevolent Society lent its grounds for circuses. Theatres took up residence in the nearby Haymarket area and around the southern end of George Street, encouraged in this location by the proximity of the railway. The International Exhibition, held in the Domain in 1879–80 was not too far away for the energetic to walk to, if the money for the fare on the new-fangled tram from Redfern Station was not available. There, in the vastness of the Garden Palace, they could observe all the wondrous inventions of modern society and forget for a while the very real shortcomings of their own urban environment. The boomtime economy of the 1880s and the overall increase in size of Sydney provided an ever-increasing range of urban entertainments which could be participated in directly, or observed from the outside.

This site housed a Bank of NSW (Westpac) from 1860. This 1894 building ceased operating as a bank in 2000.

The old chapel of the City Mission in Queen Street, now a workshop.

Cardinal Gilroy and other old boys at St Benedict's 75th anniversary, 1950.

After the building of the Blackfriars School, Chippendale got no more grand buildings to match it, although it was a period for building grandly in Sydney. There were some solid additions to the building stock, however. The Bank of New South Wales constructed an interesting building on its site at the corner of Regent Street in 1893–94. The Sydney City Mission, outgrowing the house in Paradise Row, built a Mission Church in Queen Street in 1889, where it operated for another six decades.[25] And St Benedict's, far from fading away, grew steadily larger. In 1882 Mayor Harris had inspected this school and reported it to be one large room, with boys divided from girls by an 'extremely dirty' green baize curtain. Soon after that, a convent and separate girls' school was added to the property, and in the 1890s all these buildings were replaced with a larger complex. According to the 1896 assessment the school and convent were two storeyed, with later assessments recording three storeys. If the building did not match the splendour of the Blackfriars School, it did now complement it in style and dimensions.

---

25 June Owen, *The Heart of the City*, p 72.

The number of people who ever lived or worked in Chippendale is dwarfed by the number whose association with the district was through the St Benedict's church or school or both. One of 'St Benno's' many well known pupils who attended the school in the last decade of the nineteenth century was Frank Clune, journalist and historian, who has recorded some of his remembered childhood experiences of the area. In the 1890s, he recalled, the Blackwattle Swamp Creek had not completely disappeared, and he and his friends Norman Gilroy and Harold Horder, both fellow St Benedict's pupils, often caught 'tiddlers' in the swamp. Harold Horder later became a famous footballer, while Norman Gilroy eventually became Cardinal Gilroy, Archbishop of Sydney. As a child Gilroy lived for some time in Myrtle Street, and Gilroy's mother had been a Slattery, also of Chippendale, while his aunt Theresa Slattery had married Charles Shepherd, who was descended from the Shepherd who had owned the flour mill in Abercombie Street in earlier decades. When Gilroy went back to St Benedict's as a priest it was like coming home. [26]

On other occasions, Clune would pay a visit to the Cyclorama on George Street West:

This marvellous spectacle, imported from America, showed the Battle of Gettysburg. The price of admission for kids was threepence. It was a still-life painting of a huge landscape scene, painted on canvas and faked with mirrors or magnifying devices, so that it showed the scene of the battle in what appeared to be a perspective of many acres. It had me completely tricked. After gazing at it enthralled, I would rush out to the back expecting to find the fields of Gettysburg in Harris Street, Ultimo. Then I sadly realized that it was all a mirage.

Almost as exciting and much more real must have been the sight of cows being driven down George Street West to Inglis's saleyards which were only removed to less populated parts to make way for the new Central Railway, opened in 1906. Horses, numerous in a city the size of Sydney, were also bought and sold at Inglis's. Auctions were held daily of cattle brought in the evening before, and

Knowing this, boys from Surry Hills, Ultimo, Chippendale and other suburbs arrived at the crack of dawn with a billy-can, for free milk; and many a time my three brothers and I managed to get four billies of milk to take home to help the frugal household budget. [27]

Similar household savings would have been achieved by frequenting the markets, at first in the Haymarket, and then by Darling Harbour. Manure for gardens could be had at places like Inglis's or the yards of the large omnibus company in nearby Glebe, and timber for heating coppers and creating make-do furniture from the brewery, which made its own crates and casks.

Boys were more free to participate in these rambling activities than their sisters, and sport, much of it unstructured and locally generated, was still a male preserve. The women

---

26 Frank Clune, *Saga of Sydney* (1961), p 161; Personal communication Rev. Fr E. A. Shepherd, Killara, 1988.
27 Clune, op. cit. pp 157, 160.

Blackfriars staff, 1919–22.

From an Education Department photograph labeled 'Dance Steps, Blackfriars', c.1913.

and girls could line the harbour to cheer for the favoured sculler of the day, and no doubt many of them joined the crowd of 170,000 who lined George Street outside St Andrew's Cathedral in 1889 to watch the funeral procession of Harry Searle, hero of this sport, and champion of 'the world', but opportunities for active participation were limited.

The fact of girls' restricted access to sporting and physical activities was gradually viewed as a problem in the new century, and it was in Chippendale that something began to be done about it at an official level. In 1906 the Blackfriars School had been equipped with the first serious kindergarten provided by the Education Department, and became the centre for innovation in the methods of teaching young children. Under the headmistresship of Martha Simpson, Montessori methods were introduced into the school, and the Department was impressed enough to send her overseas to study with Madame Montessori in Rome. The approach emphasised flexibility in teaching and encouraged spontaneity, creativity and self-direction in the children, with emphasis on physical movement. In this atmosphere of experimentation, the school, in co-operation with the City Council, established a playground in Victoria Park, which teachers from the school supervised. Similarly Miss Stevens, the infants mistress, in 1918 established an after-school play centre for young children and older girls to provide opportunities for 'play, organized games, rhythmic work and folk dancing'. This might not have been quite in the league of boys' activities, but it was an advance on the more sedentary ways which dominated many girls' lives. [28]

28 J. J. Fletcher, *Blackfriars Public School*, pp 10–13.

One place where both sexes could enjoy recreation was the Glaciarium, which followed the Cyclorama on George Street West. It opened its doors in 1907 and was run for many years by Dunbar Poole, 'a manager in the Edwardian tradition, decorous and courteous when formality was needed, elegant in his own way, with his high long collar and his black cravat', according to one remembrance of him. A keen amateur artist, he decorated the ice rink with make-believe Swiss scenery, and was often seen at the side of the rink, cigarette between his lips, head tilted to the side watching the skaters through a haze of smoke, intent on spotting talent and encouraging excellence. The rink produced some of the day's best skaters, but it was also a place for social gatherings and hopeful romances, and Poole, 'never preoccupied with brilliance . . . had a special softness for the "bunnies", the slow and inept beginners'. [29]

Swimming was a popular sport, especially in the early twentieth century. The closest baths were at the Natatorium, enclosed salt water pools in the basement of the Grand Natatorium Hotel in Pitt Street. It was here in the 1890s that the New South Wales Amateur Swimming Association was established. Outdoors, there were the Pyrmont Baths, built by the Council in 1875, but with the growing pollution of the harbour they had fallen into disrepair. All this changed after the new sewage outfall at Bondi came into operation in the 1890s, taking effluent out to sea. The harbour still received a lot of stormwater, but it undoubtedly became much more pleasant for swimming. The baths were refurbished and extended in 1902 and did a roaring trade, mostly from male patronage. Women were permitted to use them exclusively for only four and a half hours a week until about World War I, when 'Continental bathing (mixed)' was allowed on Wednesday evenings. [30]

Children playing in Harkness Lane (Beaumont Street) stop to watch the photographer, 1909.

Much life was lived on the street for children who played there, but also for women. They purchased many household goods from itinerant traders and passed what little spare time they had in neighbourly company. In this respect life would have been quite different from that in the more private middle class suburbs.

Mrs Edith Hughes, who moved to Goold Street as a small child in the first decade of the twentieth century, was part of what might be called a 'respectable' family, and her recollections tell of a strongly home-based life, with 'home' including always the activities of the street. The memories tell of humdrum rhythms and clear allegiances: 'everybody

29 *SMH*, 11 September 1954.

30 Michael Matthews, *Pyrmont and Ultimo: A History* (self published, 1982), p 87; NSW Gov. Gazette Vol VI, p 8270, 14 November 1902.

went to church on Sunday' and 'politics was mostly Labor'. Her father, who worked as a boilermaker's assistant at Garden Island, would catch the tram home, up George Street:

> *My father came home from work filthy dirty and had to have a bath and he'd put on another shirt and go down and get a pint of beer and bring it home. A jug cost sixpence . . . that's what he done all the week. Then of a Saturday he'd get a quart bottle, and he'd have that through Sunday. My father never hung round the hotel, but he liked to drink.*

Her mother, who thought it would have been good to move to the suburbs, took pride in her housework and the rearing of her ten children. Pinnies (aprons) were always starched, and school clothes were always changed after school was over. Sunday dinner was always hot, but not at the expense of ever missing Mass at St Benedict's, and 'the kitchen used to be washed out of a Sunday before dinner was served'. In the afternoons, still wearing good clothes, there would be a visit, by tram, to an aunt's place for tea.

Meals were often determined by the patterns of the street vendors—the rabbito, the watercress and celery man who came on Saturdays, and 'Friday, of course, was fish':

> *We'd buy it in the street. There was the ice underneath and the teatowel over it. It was all very nice and clean. They'd buy it at the fishmarket and they'd come round about nine o'clock.*

Many other purchases were done in the street, from clothes prop men, council boys selling horse manure for the 'nice little gardens', the ice man, the bottle-o. Shopping was done at the 'marvellous shopping centre' on George Street West, but not at the markets—they were reserved for the less reputable poor. Best of all, Mrs Hughes remembers going to Podesta's Icecream Factory, down Goold Street from her home, with a jug to be filled for threepence. A further penny bought wafers to complete the family treat.

Skipping and playing marbles or rounders in the street were usual and safe enough for boys and girls because traffic was slow and not very frequent. In Chippendale it was mostly of the working variety: carts rumbling out of the brewery gates pulled by the big bay horses they stabled on the grounds; the lightweight baker's cart pulled by an obedient horse; the carts of Arnolds; the monumental masons on Regent Street with a back entrance into Goold Street. The occasional funeral procession gave variety to the day, and so did the occasional procession of elephants slowly ambling down to the railway for transportation to the country circus circuit. And then, once a week according to Mrs Hughes, there was the man from Mitchell and Cranstone collecting the rent, who always drove down Goold Street in a hansom cab, a stark contrast to the more utilitarian street vehicles.

Mrs Hughes's memories did not include unpleasant scenes of domestic tensions born of poverty, although, on reflection, there was one man in the street who shot his wife dead and she did know boys who got sent to the government training ship, the *Sobraon*, for 'getting into strife'. Nor did she recall the heartbreak of housing demolitions or evictions, although 'the brewery wasn't half that size when we were there'. For many other people though, the realities included these insecurities and disruptions, especially in the second decade of the twentieth century.

By the time the Blackfriars Estate scandal had blown over, the economy was experiencing a depression of great severity. While the full impact of this was not felt until the early years of the 1890s, the building trade was in the doldrums several years earlier than this. The reasons for the depression were various. There had been too much short term borrowing for public spending in areas with very little short term returns. There had been an over-reliance on the export of wool, until the market was glutted and prices crashed. And there had been an urban real estate bonanza, fuelled by a rapidly growing population and high rate of immigration which had subsequently slowed down, leaving investors with excess property which they could not shift. Fortunes made in the seventies and eighties were now lost. The rich went bankrupt, or committed suicide, or quietly consolidated and bided their time. The clergy conducted special services for forgiveness. The poor tightened their belts, fell behind in paying the rent and shared accommodation. Housing in places like Chippendale, much of which was rented, became even shabbier than before.

Lord Mayor Taylor . . . who wanted factories.

From these events, the incipient town planning movement in Sydney drew strength. Those who believed that market forces could not be relied upon to provide decent housing for the poor were only more convinced of this in the situation of boom and slump of the late nineteenth century. Since the 1870s at least, there had been people interested in giving powers to the City Council to both demolish 'slums' (rarely defined) and to construct workers' housing. They took as their model Britain, where local authorities had become extensively involved in both demolition and construction. The Council had drafted a bill in 1902 to allow them to build workers' housing, but they were not granted this power until 1912. In the meantime, in 1905 the Council got the right to resume property in order to realign streets and to 'improve' unhealthy areas. Areas which needed 'remodelling', according to the Council, included parts of Chippendale—in the more residential areas south of the Blackfriars Estate, between Meagher and Cleveland streets, and between Smithers Street (Paradise Row) and Myrtle Street. There had been other areas of the city resumed by the Council in the years immediately following 1905, but Chippendale was to get its turn in 1911.[31]

Two years earlier, in 1909, Archdeacon Boyce of St Paul's, on Cleveland Street, had given evidence to the Royal Commission which had considered ways of improving Sydney. He suggested that Chippendale urgently needed remodelling and construction of workers' housing. It was, he said, full of 'wretched little streets' with 'no room to live'.[32]

He preached sermons about it, and took journalists on fact-finding tours and in July 1910 had been part of a deputation to see the Lord Mayor, in company with Mrs Dwyer, a

31 PC 1905, TCR pp 83–86; F. A. Larcombe, *The Advancement of Local Government in New South Wales 1906 to the Present* (1978), pp 18–21.
32 Royal Commission, *Improvement of Sydney*, 1909, p 111.

representative of the Trades Hall. 'The people ought to have better dwellings' was their straightforward message. They persuaded the Lord Mayor, Allen Taylor, to visit Chippendale, where in the company of other Council officers he 'marched to the accompaniment of a running fire of comments'. After observing 'small dilapidated tenements leaning against each other' and 'wooden structures, facetiously called cottages', according to the *Daily Telegraph* reporter, the Lord Mayor pronounced that 'they must go' which was not the same thing as saying he would provide better dwellings. Many of Chippendale's residents, appreciating the drift of things, were reported to be hostile to the Lord Mayor, and supportive of one of their number who remarked, 'Who's growling about the houses, eh? Not me.'[33]

The resumption was triggered by the knowledge that the Australian Drug Company had bought land from Thomas Dangar, a major landholder in Chippendale. The land, in Dangar Place and Myrtle Street, comprised 'various small cottages and two-story houses of

brick and stone' which were demolished to build a warehouse. This development would have blocked the continuation of Myrtle Street to Meagher Street 'for all time'. When Taylor heard of this, he personally averted it, arranging to give the company other land in exchange for a strip required for widening the road, announced the closure of Dangar Street and then, almost as an afterthought, told the Council about it. In 'this deplorable area' he observed, the Council must 'wipe away tenements which are nothing more than hovels'. He recommended the Council resume the areas illustrated, so that the place 'might be made wholesome, and cut up into decent blocks for valuable building sites for factories.' In this he probably had the support of Dangar who could see that if the Council rearranged the streets and pulled down the houses, the land—including surrounding unresumed land—would increase in value.[34] The City Health Officer, Armstrong, agreed. He said that the 358 houses involved were 'for the most part the smallest and poorest class existing in the City', some of them untenanted, and deserving of demolition. Dangar Place and

Archdeacon Boyce . . . who wanted improved housing.

Beaumont Street he found 'very squalid', while housing east of Abercrombie Street, though mixed, was very crowded. Some houses were of weatherboard, and about half were not satisfactory as habitations 'in such a city as Sydney'.[35] Given that they were in Sydney, and were inhabited, it is difficult to know just what that may have meant. Other reports recommended that the area was more suitable for commercial buildings, and by 1910 Lord Mayor Taylor, who had already presided over considerable demolitions elsewhere, had acquired a reputation for putting factories before people, commercial growth before social

33 F. B. Boyce, *A Campaign for the Abolition of the Slums in Sydney* (1913), pp 26–31.
34 *PC* 1910, LMM pp 432, 441.
35 NSCA CRS 28/2999/10 'Proposed Remodelling of Chippendale Area, 1910'—Report of Health Office, 16 September 1910.

Dangar Street . . . 'this deplorable area'. Today, it contains decrepit industrial buildings.

welfare. The Council had demolished parts of Ultimo across the road from Chippendale, and the areas of Chinese housing just north of Campbell Street in Surry Hills. The construction of new markets in Thomas Street had removed more housing. So had the Council's demolitions in Camperdown which had caused much public anger. In addition the Government had carried out resumptions for the new Central Railway. Other projects, such as the grand scheme of widening Oxford Street, and the humble scheme of widening Outram and Regent streets in Chippendale, were underway. And while some of these areas were undoubtedly unhealthy and unlovely, it began to seem to many people that a lot of the city was coming down in the first decade of the new century.

MR. SPEAKER
MEAGHER, of
N.S.W.

To men like Lord Mayor Taylor, this was the inevitable march of progress, which in his official capacity he did everything he could to foster.[36] The city, he believed, was a commercial entity, and people were far better off living in the suburbs. Many people interested in town planning agreed that suburban life was preferable to city living, but they did not all believe this could be achieved simply by demolishing houses. Others did not care so much where the housing was, as long as there was housing, and on the City Council there developed a split between Taylor's supporters, and those who were alarmed that the Council had gained the right to resume and demolish, but not to build workers' housing. The two things, they thought, should go together. By 1911, when the Chippendale

Richard Meagher, MP . . . who championed worker housing. The street behind Strickland Buildings is named after him.

36 In the *PC* for 1910 alone, there are almost 100 index entries under the heading 'Resumptions'.

15–19 Regent Street, c. 1910. The buildings are fine but the street was too narrow.

resumption was being considered by the Council, house rents in Sydney were rising rapidly, which gave credence to those who were opposed to systematic demolitions. A government select committee on 'Increase in House Rents' in 1912, listed as one of the reasons for this, the government and council demolitions.[37]

Therefore, when the Council resolved to resume parts of Chippendale in January 1911, Richard Meagher, local state member and alderman for Phillip Ward, was concerned to lead the battle for Council housing. He knew that the relevant legislation was not yet on the books, but he also understood that the cause could be advanced by tapping local resentment which was surfacing in Chippendale, as people began to be forced out of their homes. Representative was Thomas Sullivan, boilermaker, of Chippen Street, who sent this angry letter card to Meagher at Parliament House:

> *Having lived in your electorate for over 30 years and during that time have always been treated respectfully until some two months ago when the Sydney Council resumed the property…*
> 1. *How the first-thing I want to put before you is that they have gulled the tenants by stating that they would not have to leave till after the winter was over…*
> 2. *Last Monday when they came to draw the rent and was paid they gave notice to leave today, and was ejected. Their things being put out on the street if this is the way the Council does business well I am done.*[38]

The officer called upon to defend the Council's actions in this case said that it wasn't necessary to eject people, because 'when they saw that the places were rapidly being demolished they themselves quickly left the premises.' He said they did try to be considerate, but 'the instruction of the Lord Mayor . . . must be complied with.'[39]

Meagher could not stop the resumptions or the evictions, but he did harness local support for the idea of using the resumed land for housing. He did not have the numbers to get such a proposal through the Council, but by speaking at rallies he generated widespread concern for the estimated eighteen hundred people who were losing their homes. In July and August, with many houses already demolished, the Council was presented with several petitions, one signed by 600 residents, who claimed that 'the disposal of the area for factory sites' would 'practically ruin many deserving citizen':

> *It is the resident population in a locality, and the consequent ever-flowing current of human life which makes for sound and increasing values. This together with the fact of excellent drainage, and the lung spaces provided by the Parks, make it an ideal residential area.*[40]

The bit about excellent drainage was a fabrication, and the wording of the petition, with its views on what makes a city viable, indicate that it was the work of people familiar

---

37 SC, 'Increase in House Rents', *NSW V&P*, LA 1912, p 3.
38 NSCA CRS 28/2999/10, Thomas Sullivan to Richard Meagher, 22 May 1911.
39 Ibid, Comptroller to TC 31 May 1911.
40 NSCA CRS 28/2519/10, Petition to reserve Chippendale subdivision for residential purposes.

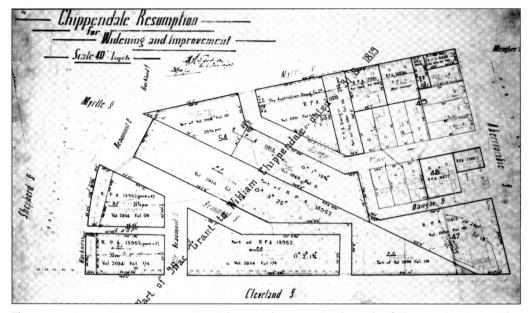

The resumption was in two main sections (*above and opposite*), either side of Abercrombie Street. This street, which had developed for housing late in the nineteenth century, contained some substantial homes. The 'after' map (*below*) of the section centred on Dangar Place shows a radically different street layout. The houses photographed in Harkness Lane and Dangar Street and hundreds more disappeared. The properties of Caleb Terrey, Elizabeth Lawler, Mary Donovan and others, whom we meet in the text, all appear on these maps. The frequency of women's names is obvious. The second section, east of Abercrombie Street, became the location of the Strickland Buildings. There was one other small section to this resumption, not included in these maps, which removed properties fronting Myrtle Street and Smithers Street, the crooked land generated by the old Paradise Row.

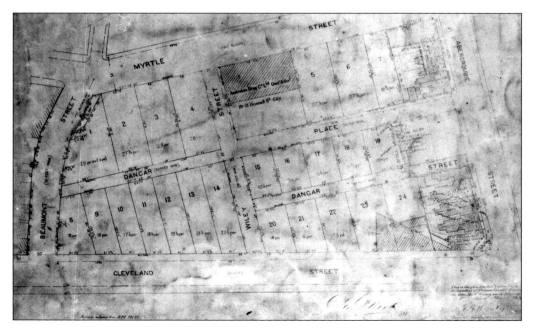

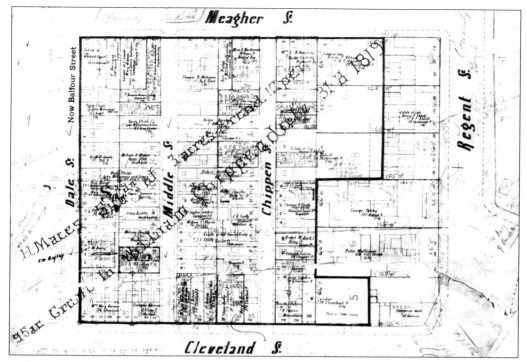

with the current town planning theories, but the signatures were of local Chippendale residents—the Lamberts, the Shepherds, the McCullas. Names appeared in pairs, in neighbouring houses, and in groups, indicating that for some families, the 'flowing current of human life' had slowed and settled in Chippendale. J. M. McCulla at 116 Myrtle Street signed it, and so did A. A. McCulla at 118 and John McCulla at 128. William McCulla wrote a letter to the Town Clerk on behalf of his widowed mother, concerned at being turned out of 123.

The first signatures on the petition were of the religious leaders of the community, including Archdeacon Boyce, who, as we have seen, in no way believed it was an 'ideal residential area'. He signed it because he believed

> It would be very unfortunate to have the city proper largely filled up with factories and the people turned out . . . It is right and wise to have a considerable number of workmen's dwellings within the city. There are men whose hours of labour are such and are so uncertain that they must live near their work. Destroyed dwellings should never be chiefly replaced by factories. [41]

This debate over what is right and wise in urban land use has continued on and off throughout the twentieth century, but in 1911 all this protest was gradually turning the tide of opinion of members of the City Council. At the end of 1911 they seesawed from

---

41 *SMH*, April 1911, quoted in F. B. Boyce, *A Campaign . . .* p 33.

agreeing to build workers' housing to accepting the Lord Mayor's position, and eventually arrived at a compromise of deciding on some council housing and some commercial development. In February 1912 the City Architect, Robert Brodrick, was instructed to draw up plans for workers' flats, and a motion to erect them was passed in March. [42] This was only a partial victory for the supporters of workers' housing, but it was something, and a first for Chippendale, which became the recipient of the first council housing built in Sydney—the Strickland Buildings. These flats, much maligned in theory by middle class reformers who advocated suburban living and detached cottages, must have been a marked improvement over the previous accommodation of their tenants. The one, two and three bedroom flats each had their own bathrooms and lavatories, with washhouses on the roofs, common garden areas and balconies. However, of the 134 planned, only half were ever build—sixty-seven flats, with four shops and four combination shop flats on the ground floor.[43] As over 350 houses had been resumed and eighteen hundred people displaced, the overall effect of 'remodelling' was depopulation.

The repercussions for Chippendale residents are preserved in the resumption records held by the City Council, which offered compensation to owners and businesses, and therefore, inevitably, was involved in protracted discussions, conferences, correspondence and court cases.[44]

Clearly, resumption did not affect everyone equally. Thomas Bayley, a bricklayer who lived in Alexandria, owned four weatherboard cottages in Dale Street which had been condemned and were standing empty at the time of resumption. He was compensated a mere £550 for the lot, and was possibly relieved to be free of the worry. Caleb Terrey, physician, of Edgecliff House, Edgecliff, was less pleased. He owned many houses in Sydney, and employed a permanent staff of tradesmen to repair and maintain them—to a minimal level of habitation, if his Chippendale properties were any guide. He owned six terraces in Chippen Street and three cottages in Middle Street. In 1910, after the inspections of Chippendale, Council ordered him to repair the Chippen Street terraces by putting in damp proof courses, cleaning the walls, repairing the roofs and guttering, renewing plasterwork, raising the kitchen ceilings to at least eight feet and lining them, paving the yards, cleaning out the closets and providing 'a sufficient water supply'. These improvements had been carried out, only to have the properties resumed. He believed he should get more compensation than he was being offered. For residents who rented these and many other properties, all they got was dislocation, stress and possibly homelessness. Perhaps the worst hit were the widows who relied on small amounts of rental for their livelihood. People who rented business premises received compensation for loss of business, but it was difficult to arrive at a proper figure. When the city solicitor said that Ethel Aldred, who rented a grocery shop in Meagher Street, wanted too much because the

---

42 *PC* 1911, LMM Chippendale Resumption 5 August 1911; *PC* 1912, LMM, 'Utilization Chippendale Resumption'. 13 December 1911; RC 15 August 1911; 21 November 1911; 26 March 1912.

43 NSCA CRS 28/2999/10; CRS 34/1511/43.

44 NSCA CRS 63, Resumption Claim Packets. Each case has a separate number. CRS 64 indexes them by name and address.

business was really very small, she replied that of course it was very small, since all the surrounding houses had been pulled down and her customers had fled. John Lawler, a bedding manufacturer who decided on reflection to call himself just a 'merchant', tried to make hay while the sun shone. Two months before the resumption he took out a twenty-one year lease on a property owned by Elizabeth Lawler, to be used as the British Motor Car Importing Company, and asked for compensation for the unexpired lease. However he had penciled across the top of the document 'property about to be resumed, lease not to be stamped'. He was sent a notice of valuation of 'nil'.

Some people, such as Jeremiah Brown, a tramways employee of Middle Street, who owned a cottage in Meagher Street, would have discovered that his title went back to William Chippendale himself; while Mary O'Brien found out that the cottage she had lived in for many years after 1873 and now rented out to Peter Donovan did not have any legal title at all. But Mary was known in the area, and she personally collected Peter's rent every week. Various people produced statutory declarations on her behalf, including Mary Donovan, who was possibly Peter's mother. She said she had lived in Chippen Street as a child in 1870s and remembered Laurence Finnigan, who had sold the property to Mary O'Brien's deceased husband, Patrick. They both recalled that for many years Finnigan had grown vegetables on the land. Mary O'Brien got her compensation. Isabella Gillard, who owned two houses in Dale Street, probably never even heard about the resumption, as she was incarcerated for insanity, and Henry Percy Owen, Master in Lunacy, handled the case.

And so the negotiation, conferences and court cases proceeded, while houses came down and people moved out and away from Chippendale. The details of the resumption tell us a lot about the area. Firstly, although most properties were rented, the landlord was more likely to be a small capitalist than a large one. The two large landlords were Thomas Dangar, who had eleven of his houses and some stables resumed, and Mary Ann Hudson of Strathfield. She owed about seventy-six houses, and received compensation to the tune of £24,000. Most landlords however owned one or two cottages, and like Hudson, many of them were women. In a world without much in the way of formalised social security, a woman with a little property was vastly more secure than one without, and it was a common method of middle class provision for old age. The likelihood of women outliving their husbands was reflected in this pattern of ownership, and also in the high numbers of widows who owned or rented shops. Probably, the poorer the area, the more likely it was that the shopkeepers would be elderly women.

As Lord Mayor Taylor had hoped, Chippendale became more industrial, and much of the resumed land was sold to factory owners. At the same time, Tooth's brewery was expanding in a large way. According to the 1896 assessment books, they had begun to buy up Wellington Street, behind the brewery, and owned about sixteen houses by 1902. By then they were also increasing ownership in O'Connor, Kensington and Abercrombie streets, with extensive inroads into Irving Street in 1906. Plans to duplicate the plant were drawn up a few years later, and these extensions were finished in 1912. The new Irving Street brewery was separated from the Kent Brewery by Balfour Street, Beyond Irving

Street corner, c. 1913.

Street, with Carlton Street intervening, was a new bottlery, replacing one that had been burnt down.[45]

The spread of factories resulted in a reduction in people, and this showed in the social life of the place. The Sydney City Mission's Sunday School and Bank of Hope lost members, although the work of the missionary William Seddon did not diminish, and in 1911 a woman volunteer, Mrs Milne, was put on as a paid worker for three days a week at fifteen shillings to help carry the load. The Mission's records tell of diminishing population, amidst extensive distributions of food parcels, clothing, boots and coal, bread and flour to those who remained.[46] The Wesleyan Chapel, which began amalgamating with other congregations in 1906 as a result of declining membership, decided to sell its property in 1915 and move operations into more populous Redfern. On 25 August 1918 the last Sunday service was held, with surrounding chapels shut for the day, to ensure that Chippendale had a congregation. And, as if to stay the execution, the local faithful held a

---

45 Tooth & Co, Ltd, *The First Hundred Years: A Brief History of Kent Brewery*, pp 35–44.
46 Sydney City Mission Minute Books, 1901–16, and *S C M Herald*, 1 September 1910; 1 August 1911
    (ML MS 4779).

final communion service on the Monday, ending with the singing of the Doxology, 'for it was seemly so to do'.[47] The chapel had stood for a mere fifty-one years, while the population had grown and then dwindled. At the Blackfriars School, the Education Department coped with the ever growing number of empty desks by using part of the building to house the Sydney Teachers College. This was set up in 1905, and in association with it, the kindergarten previously mentioned. Blackfriars' closeness to the University allowed the students to easily attend lectures up the road. The anticipated college on the campus did not materialise until after World War I, so the students' sojourn in Chippendale was a long one.[48]

Increasingly people came into Chippendale to work or study, but they lived elsewhere and owed their allegiances to other places.

---

47 G.J. Pitt, 'Wesley Church, Chippendale', *Journal of Australasian Methodist Historical Society*, Vol 11, Pt 4, No 7, July 1934, p 113.
48 J.J. Fletcher, *Blackfriars Public School*, pp 9–10.

4

FROM 1914 TO THE PRESENT

A COMPREHENSIVE HISTORY of twentieth century Chippendale would require a great deal of space. The momentous events of the century which impinged on Australian society also affected Chippendale's residents, and as the world was drawn ever closer together by more efficient communications, more of what happened elsewhere was known about, reacted to and acted upon than in earlier times. Physically, the trains and trams, and later cars, meant that people's first hand experiences of the world became wider, while the radio, motion pictures, newsreels and more recently television have all resulted in greater interaction with the rest of Sydney and the world.

Thus, when the first rumblings of war were heard in July 1914, and the first recruiting of soldiers got underway, men from Chippendale were there. But so were men from everywhere else, and so at one level there was nothing particular about this phenomenon which related to Chippendale. On the other hand, men were not recruited evenly from every suburb or social class. Along with the patriotism which motivated volunteers, there was also a rising unemployment rate in 1914, and many welcomed army service as an alternative to economic hardship. This would have been more important in a place like Chippendale than in wealthier areas. Similarly, as the turbulent events of the war years unfolded, they were received differently in different places. From the start there were pockets of anti-British and anti-war feelings especially amongst Australia's Roman Catholics of Irish descent. The most outspoken critics of the war in the IWW (International Workers of the World, known colloquially as Wobblies) were gaoled in 1915. This possibly had as much effect on the minds of some Chippendale residents as the events of Gallipoli of the same year. [1]

For others, the most important issues would have had more to do with the hunger they felt in their stomachs, as soldier-husbands neglected to remit money, and food prices rose. Before Christmas 1915 a notice went up on the rectory door at St Paul's announcing that the needy could call on Thursday, 23 December. Canon Boyce records that he intended to conduct interviews and write out grocery orders for deserving cases, but when his wife Caroline opened the door 'a great crowd of people' pushed their way inside, knocking her down. According to Boyce, the shock of this contributed to the stroke she had on Christmas night, leaving her partially paralysed. The physical and psychological toll on people who went hungry that Christmas will remain unknown.

For yet others, 1915 was the year of the early closing campaign, when a huge march proceeded from the Town Hall to Parliament House with the largest petition ever produced

---

1 For an account of Australian society during the years of World War I, see Stuart McIntyre, *The Oxford History of Australia*, Vol. IV, 1901–1942 (1986).

in Australia, in favour of six o'clock closing of the state's hotels. According to the temperance movement's literature, early closing was more needed in places like Chippendale than anywhere else, and it was first hand experiences of working in the area which moved the two local Anglican clergymen, Boyce and Hammond of St Barnabas, George Street West, to play leading roles in the campaign. But though their efforts no doubt assisted in creating a general climate which led to a sweeping victory for six o'clock closing, voters of Chippendale (Phillip Ward) did not contribute to it. With its large brewery and its many inhabitants for whom the pub was an integral part of their lives, the local vote firmly supported the liquor lobby. [2]

The 1916 Easter Rebellion in Ireland created an increase in anti-war feelings. Later in the year came the first of the referenda on conscription, and the splitting of the Labor Party. Sectarian bitterness and industrial unrest intensified by 1917, such that, according to historians of the period, the government was in a continuous state of crisis until the end of the war. [3]

To many in Chippendale these years were punctuated not only by the pain of death and injury to loved ones in the far-off European war and the tolling of the bell at St Paul's for every parish lad who fell at the front, but by Sunday sermons and street corner meetings which questioned the wisdom of it all. In August 1917 a dispute involving tramwaymen spread to the railways and other transport workers and wharf workers in what came to be almost a general strike. Violent clashes between strikers and government-

Above: Needlework teachers' exhibition, Blackfriars School, 1918.
Above right: Buckland Street demolitions, 1918.

2 F. B. Boyce, *Fourscore Years and Seven* (1934) pp 82–83; 155–63.
3 Stuart McIntyre, *The Oxford History of Australia*, Vol IV, pp 142–76.

Paramedics fighting the influenza outbreak, outside the Blackfriars Depot, 1919.

sponsored blacklegs and repressive legislation followed. For still others 1917 was the year the Council widened Buckland Street, thereby knocking their houses down. [4]

The year that hostilities ended in Europe also brought influenza. This meant more days and weeks off work, restricted movement and hardship. The emergency services set up to deal with this crisis included a depot at Blackfriars School from whence white-clad and masked paramedics set forth to do battle with this internal enemy.

The dominant factors which we may assume affected the way events were experienced in Chippendale were the working class position of most of its inhabitants and the Irish Catholic origins of many of them. There were, however, many exceptions. Unfortunately, the census material does not allow us many useful details about this area until after World War II. In 1921, twenty-four per cent of Sydney's population was Catholic, but this figure went well above thirty per cent in inner areas. Statistically, where there were large percentages of Catholics there were small percentages of Presbyterians, while Anglicans were everywhere. [5] Clearly, when people remember that 'every one was Catholic' or 'we were all Irish' they do not mean it statistically.

What is being claimed has more to do with a recognition that the mix of social and cultural values differed from the dominant values of urban Sydney.

---

4 NSCA CRS 63/1213–1217.
5 Peter Spearritt, *Sydney Since the Twenties* (1978), p 209.

The fact that Chippendale was working class needs no census figures to confirm it, as the evidence of the built environment is overwhelming. The area's twentieth century story is one of industrial and commercial ebb and flow as numerous factories and workshops grew and changed hands. Enmeshed in the fabric of Chippendale life are the experiences of workers and residents involved in food processing, printing, engineering and textiles. From the buildings of these few streets have come hats and caps, shoes and corsets, cake mixes and chocolate bars, newspapers and high quality printing jobs, castings and metal products too numerous to relate.

By the time of World War I the ground rules for land use had been set, determined in part by the nature of the area itself, in part by the political decisions of the City Council that this was a proper place for industrial activities. As pressure built up in the inner city for commercial and retailing space, the next places out from the centre took over industrial functions, and none more intensely than Chippendale. The related idea, that people would be better off living in suburbia, was loudly voiced, and created one more reason why people in places like Chippendale were 'different' from the metropolitan 'norm'. This pressure to migrate to the suburbs was psychological as much as physical. People reacted to it by moving out, or dreaming of moving out, or distancing themselves from what bourgeois commentators claimed was unacceptable behaviour in those who still lived in the city. 'Three things I am proud of', recalled Laura McCrae who began raising children in a house in Abercrombie Street in the 1920s, 'I never had a visit from a policeman, a bad report from a school or a cross word from a neighbour'—here was respectability, surburban style, against all odds. Mrs McCrae, a gently spoken lady well into her second century when I spoke to her in 1987, was the Mayoress of Redfern for a time, and was widely known and respected in Chippendale where she worked for many years as a volunteer at the Council's Activity Centre. Others valued the good things of inner city living, and despite the weight of public opinion against them, stubbornly remained, with house and factory uneasily vying with each other for precious space in congested Chippendale. Part of the story of the twentieth century is of the slow and gradual victory for industry, part is of the resilience and energy of residents. Open confrontation between the two interested groups has been only occasional, but the battle of the residents against a pervasive community judgement that they were anachronistic and unimportant in the modern city of commuters from leafy suburbs has been continuous. The intensity of antagonism towards residential living in areas like Chippendale has varied, and gradually, over the decades, the battlers have moved out and away. In recent decades however the tide of opinion has turned somewhat, and the positive qualities of inner city living have become widely canvassed. For some people in Chippendale—and there are some whose Chippendale connections go back many generations—living there has always been valued.

Population figures are not readily available, although there are some for Phillip Ward for the late nineteenth century, and the same area can be extracted from the latest census. These give the information shown in Table 1. The 1986 figure has been calculated by combining census districts to cover the same area as the nineteenth century figures. By 1986, in a city largely depleted of people, Phillip Ward had reduced its proportion of city

Table 1: POPULATION, PHILLIP WARD*

	M	F	T	% of City population
1861	2764	3151	5915	10
1871	3922	4232	8154	11
1901	6981	5572	12,553	11
1986	1283	805	2008	4

* Chippendale and part of Surry Hills.

population to a mere four per cent. Of the 12,553 people who lived in Phillip at the turn of the century, perhaps 10,000 lived in Chippendale. By 1944 a government survey of factory workers estimated that 10,000 worked in the same area.

Of the 2,008 people living in 'Phillip' in 1986, 1,537 lived in Chippendale. But lower figures were recorded in 1976 and 1981. These figures demonstrate, in a tentative way, the beginnings of a return to living in what had almost ceased to be an industrial suburb and become an industrial estate.

Many people's reminiscences about life in Chippendale begin with sounds that evoke a rich industrial history; the clacking of knitting machines; the chipping of monumental masons; the clopping of horses returning and leaving the brewery or the Post Master General's yards in Myrtle Street; the clanging of heavy machinery.

More strongly and more often people recall smells. Early on, there was the smell of the steam trams and trains, of horses and gas lights. But those were smells general to Sydney. Overlaying these were Chippendale's own smells. Of longest duration and least fondness was the brewery, with the oppressively cloying smell of the hops. Then there was Fostars Shoe Factory which began in the late 1920s in a small way in Abercrombie Street, then moving to Balfour Street where it operated until 1958 on a site since taken over by the brewery. 'I can never think of Chippendale without smelling the sweet smell of leather'. Sweeter still were the tempting smells of confectionery being produced at numerous locations. The White Wings cake factory in Meagher Street (until 1982) had different baking days—vanilla days, orange days, chocolate days, while 'kids would walk past the MacRobertson's factory just for a smell of Cherry Ripe.' As one resident put it, 'Chippendale did not so much have weather, as smells'.[6]

The kinds of activities which Chippendale would sustain for most of the twentieth century were well in place by the time World War I was over and the city was on the verge of a few years of buoyant economic expansion before the depression of 1929 set in. A survey of the buildings and occupations listed in *Sands Directory* for 1921 shows that although the individual firm names would not necessarily last, the kinds of activities pursued would prove

---

6 Text in quotations comes from personal reminiscences and the source is only acknowledged specifically where it seems appropriate. A list of people who talked to me about Chippendale is in the Acknowledgements.

Grace Bros, Broadway . . . 'that is how I came to leave Grace Brothers. They gave me blouses to make. They were getting 9s or 10s in the shop from them, and from my book I saw I was only getting 9d'. (Mary Edwards, evidence to 'Royal Commission on Female Labour . . .', 1911–12, p 39).

durable. Clothing manufacture was firmly ensconced, in places like the Monarch Shirt Factory (corner of Rose and Cleveland Streets), the Roslen Shirt Factory (Cleveland Street), Robert Reid and Company (Balfour Street), and W.A. Davidson (Blackfriars Street). Crosby House, a five storey building on George Street West—one of the few which had fulfilled the predictions of the purveyors of land on the Blackfriars Estate for more substantial buildings on this street—had all its floor space taken up by the rag trade. In addition there were several small clothing factories on City Road, hatmakers in Carlton Street, the Omar Knitting Company (Abercrombie Street) and Macrae's Knitting Company in Regent Street. Here too was Anthony Hordern's embroidery factory, while Grace Brothers had a tailoring factory in Knox Street.

Hordern's and Grace Brothers were two of Sydney's largest department stores in the era when department stores were larger and more dominant in retailing than they later became. Grace Brothers had been trading on George Street West since 1886, and in 1906 opened a grand new store, while Horderns, long on Brickfield Hill, had built a new and grand emporium which opened in 1905. Both of these stores employed about 3,000 people each in the early 1920s, and as both were close to Chippendale they played a role in its history, as places both to shop and to work. But in addition to these stores, and similar ones, like Marcus Clark's, located from 1906 to 1924 at the junction of Pitt and George streets, where the toll gate once stood, and then on George Street West, they provided large employment in their factories and workshops producing a large range of house brand products.[7]

Other manufacturers with long Chippendale associations were in place by the end of

---

7 Howard Wolfers, 'The Big Stores Between the Wars' in Jill Roe (ed) *Twentieth Century Sydney* (Sydney, 1980), pp 18–33.

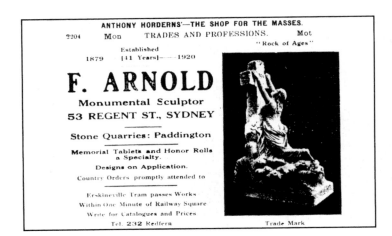
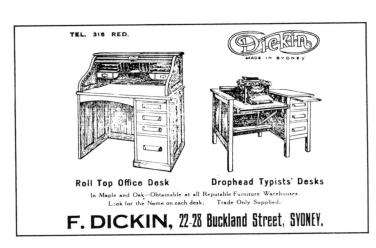

Kent Brewery staff, 1935.

World War I. The food processing industry was there in the form of the Bendollar Chocolate Company in Abercrombie Street, the large cereal foods manufacturer H.L. Bussell and Company in Meagher Street (later to become White Wings), the warehouses of the wholesale grocers Moran and Cato, MacRobertson's chocolate factory and the Phoenix Biscuit Factory, all on Cleveland Street. Podesta's, remembered by Mrs Hughes who lived in Goold Street before the war, were still making ice cream, while the wafers they sold to go with it possibly came from the cone and wafer manufacturer in O'Connor Street. Boots were made at several locations and furniture in at least half a dozen different workshops. Heavy manufacturing was represented in both wholesaling and production spheres by firms like Clutterbuck Brothers, machinery merchants of City Road, several wire workers, spring makers and galvanisers, as well as those who called themselves engineers, such as Lewis, Ricketts Murdoch and Company (Meagher Street), Arnold and Company (O'Connor Street) and Robinson Brothers (Knox Street). A long term Chippendale occupant was the printing industry. This included Simpsons Ink Ltd in Blackfriars Street, Butterfield and Lewis's printery in Shepherd Street and the offices and works of the *Land* newspaper in Abercrombie Street.

The 'new' industries in Sydney in the 1920s were concerned with electricity and motor vehicles. Neither had very much direct impact on Chippendale's residents, for although they benefited from brighter street lighting, which arrived in 1904, as yet they could neither afford nor accommodate the new-fangled electrical appliances. Long after the twenties, people recall collecting wood from the brewery to heat coppers and stoves, and in the 1940s the installation of chip heaters for heating bath water was considered 'a luxury, gee whiz'. Many continued with gas lighting way beyond the arrival of electricity, and although the motor car population burgeoned in the twenties, cars in Chippendale were mostly just passing through. Electricity did enter the workshops more rapidly, and being on several major transit routes out of the city, Chippendale soon attracted related industries. In 1921 there was the Dalwood Brothers motorcycle works in Regent Street, the Electric Lamp Repairing Company in Daniels Street, motor accessories manufacturers in Meagher Street and the Repatriation Motor Body Building School in Queen Street, as well as various garages and agents for car firms.

Chippendale also produced perambulators and brushes, tombstones and oilskins, artificial flowers and musical instruments, agricultural sprays and chemicals. Wholesalers of lime and cement on Regent Street near the railway, tea merchants on George Street West, packing stores and showrooms complete the 1921 list of manufacturing activities in Chippendale.

What the directory did not list were the many workshops contained within the premises of the Kent Brewery, by far the largest employer in Chippendale. Here was a whole world of tradesmen making almost all of the requirements of the plant. The company expanded substantially in the 1920s and 1930s, although there must have been some anxious moments in 1928 when the prohibition movement had rallied enough strength to take the people to a referendum on the question of banning production and sale of alcohol. The vote went firmly in favour of the demon drink. By 1935 there were

'Smoko' at the brewery, 1935.

1300 workers at Tooths, a few of them uniformed women working the offices. According to a brewery publication, there were sixty-one different 'callings' being carried out. These included unskilled carters and lumpers of grain, coal, sugar and barrels, skilled coopers, painters making advertising signs, sailmakers making tarpaulin covers for delivery trucks, smiths, chemists and laboratory technicians. [8]

The urban boom of the twenties did not pass unnoticed in Chippendale, and although unemployment did not disappear, there was increased opportunity for work locally. This was especially true for women, as factory employment in clothing and food production increased. The extra shillings no doubt saw their way back into households which rejoiced at the lifting of war time restriction on household goods, as well as into the tills of the booming department stores and the box offices at 'the movies'. St Benedict's School got a large extension, and the state premier, Jack Lang, opened a remodelled Dispensary in Regent Street in 1926. This would have made basic medical care a little more accessible to those unable to afford private doctors' fees.

Meanwhile, the steady substitution of factories for homes continued, taking a house here, a row there. Interest in slum clearance subsided as prosperity led to a naïve hope that 'the problem' of inadequate housing would wither away, but at the same time an upsurge of interest in better city traffic management resulted in continued house demolitions. By the early 1920s, motor vehicles outnumbered horse drawn vehicles in Sydney, with the most rapid increase being in motor lorries. [9] To the increase in traffic there was added the chaos of the intermingling of the old and the new, with horses, trams, motor buses, horse-drawn drays, vans and motorised trucks all converging on the city. The road rules were minimal and the authorities had little experience with traffic flow control.

Several grand schemes for widening major roads were embarked upon, including the widening of George Street West—from Railway Square to Regent Street by realignment, and from there to City Road by resumption. This involved many small shops and workshops, several hotels and a few substantial buildings—the E. S. and A. Bank, Crosby House and St Benedict's Church. [10]

Back in 1911 when other parts of Chippendale had been resumed, many people had experienced what they felt was rapid upheaval and sudden disruption to their lives as demolitions followed hard on the heels of resumption. By the twenties, with more experience behind it, the City Council had learned to take things more slowly. Resumed properties were customarily re-leased to their current tenants until demolition could occur, usually in blocks, and not until widening was imminent. This reduced the stress on tenants and reduced the amount of compensation the Council had to pay. In addition, owners of resumed properties could be offered alternative sites from resumption land residues or other council properties in lieu of financial compensation. These practices could all make a resumption less disruptive. However, in the case of the widening of

---

8 Tooth & Co. Ltd, *The First Hundred Years: A Brief History of Kent Brewery* (1935), pp 69–87 describes the processes at that date.

9 Peter Spearritt, *Sydney Since the Twenties*, op. cit pp 119, 159–60.

10 NSCA CRS 34/4535/24 'Minute Paper—George Street West Widening Resumption—Leasing etc.'

The Dispensary, Regent Street, opened in 1926. The earlier building, a refurbished house, began dispensing advice and medicines in 1871.

George Street West, things progressed at a snail's pace with tenants and owners caught in a web of indecision.

The project, which had seemed like a good idea in the prosperous years of 1925–26, had become ensnared in both the administrative disruptions at the Town Hall, where the Council was sacked in 1927 and replaced by state-appointed commissioners, and in the economy's downturn. It was not until the 1940s that the widening was completed. Some of the more complex resumption settlements dragged on and on. Abraham Aboud, the owner of Crosby House, finally settled on a plan which involved exchanging the front portion of his building for a sideways extension after demolition of several other properties. Numbers 128–134 George Street West were auctioned to demolishers in October 1933 and Aboud took vacant possession of the land in November. He was given until August 1934 to demolish the front part of his building back to the new building line, but, after all the years taken to reach settlement, he was not inclined to oblige. Neither did he respond to a letter from the Council requesting that he demolish in time for the road to be widened for the forthcoming royal visit of the Duke of Gloucester in November. This was probably not prompted by any anti-royalist feelings, but by the observation that other buildings still straddled the new building line of the street. [11]

The longest and most complicated resumption settlement was with St Benedict's, which was not finalised until the early forties. The church administration paid only a peppercorn rent for its building from the date of resumption until negotiations commenced in seriousness in 1936. Four years and two acts of parliament later the enormously expensive option of compensating for demolishing the church had been rejected in favour of reinstating the building on the site. The widening took twenty-six feet of land, and required that the church be shortened by about two thirds of this amount. It also took a small slice of the presbytery next door. The original claim, for pulling it down, was £127,000. The final settlement, arrived at towards the end of 1938, was for just over £40,000. Clearly reinstatement was a preferable option for the Council and was accepted by the church because it was not likely to be in a position to build a replacement church in anything like the grand original style. St Benedict's was not a prosperous parish and it was determined to get the compensation due to it. Apart from reconstructing the front of the church to the original design, so that in future years no one would know it had been shortened, the claim included other items concerned with its dislocation, some of which may have surprised the humble parishioners of Chippendale who dutifully placed their hard-earned shilling on the plate on Sundays. Dismissing the idea that the parish priests could find any suitable accommodation in the area, the list of claims included hotel accommodation for sleeping and sitting rooms for the priests during building operations, and in addition, accommodation for a valet as 'the three priests have always been accustomed to valet services'. [12]

On settlement in September 1938 the Council indicated that it would like the site of the road widening to be cleared within three months, but the church argued that it could not legally be made to move until the act of parliament necessary to permit reinstatement of the building was passed. By now St Benedict's was causing a bottleneck, with the buildings on both sides of it long since demolished, and this did not enhance its community image. By mid-1939 the Council was receiving some rather terse correspondence from the Loyal Orange Lodge suggesting that the church was being given preferential treatment, compared to the local businessmen who had been disrupted unnecessarily early, it now seemed. By the end of the year the act was assented to and demolitions begun, though rebuilding was not completed until as late as August 1941 when Roy Hendy, the Town Clerk, wrote to Dean Norris at St Benedict's pointing out that the widening of Broadway could still not be finalised because of slow progress on the

---

11 NSCA CRS 63/1563; 63/1590.
12 NSCA CRS 63/1620.

The transport revolution in the twenties. The first photo, taken about 1920, shows carts and horses and lorries vying for dominance in the brewery yard. In the second, George Street West, taken from Grace Bros tower in 1930, only three carts are visible.

building. It is not known how Hendy had responded to the formal notification from the Dean in late 1939 that there were 'some rather good magnolia trees on the resumed area. The Council could have these for cost of removal'. Perhaps after all this, the Town Clerk would not have been fond of magnolia trees.

The end result was a road over one hundred feet wide, including footways, called Broadway, the name which the department store Grace Brothers had been using for their part of the street for many years previously. Back in 1879 when the Blackfriars Estate was advertised for sale, the estate agents had offered a vision of a grand row of commercial buildings here, but it had not happened. Four decades on, in the urban expansion of the 1920s the same transformation was hoped for, but again it did not happen, as prosperity proved transitory, and depression set in. The old buildings are mostly still there, testimony to austere times of the 1930s and 1940s. The removal of the row of shops in front of the Kent Brewery left a blank industrial wall to front Broadway, and in a few places residues of land were still unbuilt on in the 1980s, being used as car lots. St Benedict's did not use the opportunity to open itself out to an entrance from this new road, but conserved as much length as it could. The plain wall fronting the road contains no doors, and windows are meshed over to protect against possible destruction from passing traffic. The front face of Chippendale was not uplifted by this city 'improvement' and increasingly it became a place to be merely passed by. This was reinforced by the demise of the big department stores in the Railway Square precinct.

Grace Brothers completed its new grand store in 1928–29, but it was not the trading success of its rivals further downtown like Farmers or Mark Foys, and the survival of the firm was probably due to a 1933 decision to decentralise to suburban locations. The other grand local store, Marcus Clark's, just faded away, with the building being recycled as a technical college. The shift of trading away from this area was tied to the growth of private car ownership, which reduced dependence on Central Railway Station, and the opening of the underground railway, which carried passengers closer to the centre of town. St James

St Benedict's with magnolia trees, 1926. It looked the same, if shorter, after resumption and rebuilding.

and Museum stations were opened in time for Christmas 1926, with Town Hall and Wynyard stations following in 1933.[13]

The Depression years, officially the early 1930s, are not easy to pinpoint in terms of severity or duration, but in places like Chippendale came early and lasted longer than in more prosperous areas. Unemployment levels, based on official trade union figures, were of the order of thirty per cent of the male workforce at the height of the depression in 1933, with about one fifth out of work from mid-1930 to the end of 1934. In some working class areas some estimates put it at forty per cent. But many men in Chippendale never worked in anything like regular work or got anywhere near belonging to a union, and for these it would have been a case of less work, more erratic work, more intensification of underemployment and black market employment. Young people were the most likely to be out of work, while women were perhaps the least. This was because women's employment was disproportionately located in low-paid, basic commodity production, such as took place in the food and clothing factories of Chippendale. However, these too cut back on production, and their very concentration in inner city areas meant that inner city girls and women who relied heavily on this kind of work to supplement meagre household incomes were disadvantaged.[14] As much as income was needed, it was ingrained in many people's thinking that men were the 'natural' breadwinners, and enormous stress was generated in many household where this didn't happen.

73 O'Connor Street, 1934. Evictions meant finding somewhere else, or doubling up. One of a series of photographs taken by the City Council to record the illegal use of verandahs as rooms.

13 Peter Spearritt, *Sydney Since the Twenties*, pp 225–26.
14 Stuart McIntyre, *The Oxford History of Australia*, Vol IV, p 275.

Neilson Slipper Factory, Broadway, 1945. Women's labour was essential to 'the war effort'.

It is easy to romanticise the Depression in areas like Chippendale. Strong community and family ties are often assumed to have substituted for work and adequate nourishment, and morale is often remembered as being higher than in more atomised middle class suburban areas. Perhaps it was. Not many had to worry about share prices, which were irrelevant to their lives. And though nobody relished the idea of lining up at a soup kitchen, when the line contained so many neighbours who were clearly in the same predicament, it was easier to blame the system and not yourself. Perhaps. People certainly remember great acts of neighbourly generosity verging on heroism.

No doubt individual responses varied enormously, ranging from self-contained efforts at maintaining respectability at all costs to out-and-out lawlessness, from total emotional collapse to defiant attacks against the system which had produced this economic shambles. It is the defiant whose memories make the best stories—like those of Sonny Glynn, who was a youth when the bailiff came to evict his parents from their house in O'Connor Street. As he recalled it, his father and his mates were inside the house with the doors and windows locked, and his mother was being protected at a neighbour's house:

Next minute this bloke comes and he's got a copper with him . . . 'Come on, open up'.
Then it starts, all the crowd arrives, and starts pelting them. The young copper 'e says,

'It's got nothin' to do with me. I'm only 'ere to protect 'im'. 'If you won't come out', [the bailiff] says, 'then the door's goin' in.' So 'e starts cuttin' part of the door, so 'e can get 'is hand in. Well 'e wasn't a very intelligent bailiff because when 'e made the break, and put 'is 'and in, that's when the world fell in on 'im.

The rest of the story is a triumph of community solidarity. The men inside crashed a pick handle down across the bailiff's arm, the jubilant crowd enjoyed the spectacle of him dancing around in agony, the young policeman failed to take any action to support the bailiff, and eventually the landlord agreed to let the family stay on in the house, paying the rent when they could—and usually they couldn't.

Behind the apparent spontaneity of this episode were indications of a well-organised campaign. The men were in the house, barricading it, the women were safely away, and the crowd was at the ready to do battle with a bailiff who was clearly expected. Although it was not mentioned, the events suggest the backing of the Unemployed Workers Movement, which mounted a stubborn campaign against house evictions from late 1930 onwards. This one, one of about two hundred successful campaigns, was probably early in

Victoria Park, across the road from Chippendale—a haven for children and lovers. The photograph shows a council worker clearing reeds, 1930.

the history of the movement, because later events were often violent and police took an active role in assisting in the evictions.[15]

The success of these anti-eviction battles was partly explained by the likely consequences if an eviction did occur. Then the neighbours and erstwhile tenants would move in quickly and strip the house of anything of value. 'When they threw people out,' recalled Mavis Kenny, 'they'd tear up the floor, get the lead off the roof. Gas fittings, coppers out the back . . . anything they could get a few bob for.' With the increasing difficulty of finding replacement tenants as the Depression deepened, it made more sense for landlords to leave residents in the houses, even if they could not pay, rather than risk such destruction of their property.

Many people were unprepared to involve themselves in these methods of survival, and many houses did become empty. So too did some factories, like that of John Danks and Son Limited in Buckland Street. Here the Reverend Robert Hammond set up one of several 'Hammond Hotels' as emergency accommodation. The factory, which is visible in the photo on page 96, was rented at eight pounds per week, an amount which did not even cover normal outgoing expenses. Guests who were single men handed over their dole coupons valued at seven-and-six a week—nobody stayed for free—and for this they received a bed, hot meals, and facilities for washing and ironing clothes, in order to maximise their chances of success when they went looking for work. The dining hall, recently an industrial shed, contained a piano, wireless, library books and a screen for showing pictures on Tuesday nights. To these many locals came, and while the 'hotel' had beds for thirty, often about three hundred attended for meals.

This was only one of many examples of Hammond's down-to-earth approach to his ministry. St Barnabas' Church on George Street West, where he was rector from 1918 until his retirement in 1943, was described as combining 'the offices of an employment bureau, a restaurant, a barbering establishment, a bootmending business, a metal workshop, a Christian fellowship . . .'[16]

He set up an emergency depot where men could iron, get a button sewn on, get a train fare. The 'Positions Vacant' columns of the *Herald* were pasted up inside the church gates, while the weekly messages emblazoned on the large billboard outside urged manly resistance to the forces of despair, with sentiments like 'cut your own wood; it will warm you twice.' A political conservative and firm believer in self help, Hammond gathered around him a large band of workers who laboured tirelessly to alleviate the worst excesses of the suffering of the Depression years. According to his biographer he was not an easy man to get along with, often moody, often brusque or, as some saw it, rude, unable to suffer fools gladly. And neither did he make any secret of his contempt for inner city living. His biggest achievement was the establishment of Hammondville, a self help settlement on the rural fringes of Sydney, where people contributed to building homes they would eventually buy, on land donated and scrounged from wealthy citizens. These included

---

15 Nadia Wheatley, 'Meeting Them at the Door', in Jill Roe (ed), *Twentieth Century Sydney*, pp 208–230.
16 Bernard G. Judd, *He That Doeth: The Life Story of Archdeacon R. B. S. Hammond* (1951), p 208.

Strickland Buildings, constructed on resumed land in Balfour Street in 1914.

R.R. Dangar, whose family name, it might be remembered, was linked with nineteenth century wealth accrued through subdivisions of Chippendale land. Hammondville eventually reached 225 acres, and by 1937 contained one hundred cottages. Needless to say, the quality of life there was compared most favourably with that of the inner city. [17]

The movement to eradicate city 'slums' through demolition regained momentum after the Depression, but only in theory. Before anything happened in a practical way World War II was a reality, and the subject was again closed. Restrictions on house construction, rent control and 'making do' were the order of the day.

For many people the Depression continued a long time, with the whole of the 1930s being years of austerity, flowing into the lean years of the early part of the war which were to follow. Lean years and lean horses, according to the children's taunt of 'What do you feed your horses on? Clothes props?'

Ray Cowling, who was born in the Strickland Flats in 1933, remembers that as a very small child he would go to the pub with his father, where he would sit on the front step, drinking lemonade and eating pigs' trotters, which were sometimes provided as free counter lunch fare in those years. By the early forties he had moved to Pine Street, near the Allen's sweets factory, and as he remembers it,

17 Ibid, pp 20, 180–85.

*We were lucky in Chippendale. There were that many lolly factories, it was great bein'
a kid in Chippendale. Scanlens, Hoadley's MacRobertsons . . . they were all places you
went to. You sneaked up the lane and in the bins there at the back you'd go through the
tins and get all the bits of lollies and chocolates.*

It sounds like any child's heaven, but the pleasure with which these activities were
recalled is evidence of a childhood without much to spare in the way of material things.
With his mates, he would go to the gates of the railway workshops after school, and wait
for the men to come off their shift. 'We'd ask for "sparies", cakes and sandwiches they
didn't eat for their lunch.' Sunday afternoon fishing expeditions with his father to the Man-
o-War steps provided pleasure, but also an addition to the family table, for 'even though
there'd be about a hundred people there with lines going everywhere, Dad'd always finish
up with a feed of a Sunday night.'

The war meant many things. To Ray and his mates, it meant exploring the trenches dug
in Victoria Park in the hope of disturbing the odd drunk or furtive pair of lovers, or later,
when the United States servicemen began arriving in town, tagging them at Luna Park or
similar locations in the hope of relieving them of some of the money they were fond of
distributing. It meant following along behind the airforce apprentices, mimicking their
military swaggers, as they daily marched through Chippendale from their quarters at the
Deaf and Dumb Institute in Darlington Road to the technical college in Ultimo. It meant
occasionally accompanying his grandfather, still living in the Strickland Buildings, on his
street patrols as air raid warden, ensuring that blackouts were maintained.

For adults, there were food shortages and rations. Hotels received a quota of beer, and the
quicker they could sell it, the quicker they could close up, thereby reducing their wage bill.
Some sold their bottle quota on the blackmarket, so when the taps ran dry the men had to
go down to Surry Hills to buy more from Kate Leigh, one of the biggest dealers in sly grog.
For locals in the know 'you could always get what you needed—butter, tea, even at the little
shops. Nobody ever put them in, because if you did you were only cuttin' your own throat.'

Food, as we have seen, was always important in Chippendale, one way or another.
There may have been inadequate amounts of it in some of the houses, but the factories
were operating to capacity. This was especially so after Japan entered the war. From the
start munitions factories had taken on many women workers, but with the stationing of
troops in the Pacific, there was a need for production to expand in the more traditional
areas of women's work. The troops needed food, clothes and boots. Women were
encouraged, cajoled and finally conscripted into the factory. Those who were earning high
levels of pay in the metal sector resisted this compulsory shift which resulted in greatly
decreased wages. [18] Some found new freedom and purpose in joining the paid workforce,
some did it as a patriotic duty. But after the war was over, many were used to the life and
would not return to unpaid domesticity, no matter how much family and government
propaganda encouraged it.

---

18 For women's involvement in war work see Lynn Beaton, 'The Importance of Women's Paid Labour' in Margaret
Bevege *et al, Worth Her Salt* (1982), pp 84–98.

Map, begun in 1949, showing the predominance of industrial buildings in the northern half of Chippendale.

The opposite map dates from the early post-war period. Part of a series compiled from 1949 onwards, it located the major land uses in Chippendale from then until about the end of the 1960s. Consultation with other sources indicates that it is probably more correctly a reflection of activities in the early 1950s. Clearly the dominating industry was the brewery. During the war vast quantities of fruit juice had been produced here for the use of the forces, and some of the workshops had been tooled up to produce guns, but expansion of the traditional product was what was demanded in the prosperous fifties.[19]

The map shows a strong continuance of the industries isolated back in 1921: textiles, including the large Berlei House in Regent Street; engineering; food processing, with an emphasis on sweets; and printing. This last group had expanded greatly with at least seven establishments concerned with newspaper, business and art printing. The other expanding, though not new industry group was concerned with transport. The stabling of the Postmaster General's horses had become the garages for the same department, taking up large amounts of land in Dangar Place, and many commercial motor-servicing businesses had established themselves. Tooths had phased out the brewery draught horses from the 1930s, but maintained garages and motor workshops in the brewery complex.[20]

During the 1920s and 1930, the possibilities for low-cost entertainment and recreational pursuits increased in variety and availability over earlier times. The 'pictures' were king, with the nearest theatres in the Haymarket and Lawsons in Redfern. From the 1930s and through to the war, dance halls like the Trocadero and the Palais were popular, with many others less well known as well. There was one in City Road, a stone's throw from Chippendale, and the St Benedict's church hall was also used for dances. Entertainment of a sporting nature revolved around football and boxing. Billy McConnell's gym, first in Abercrombie Street, and by the 1950s in Pine Street, figures largely in male reminiscences. Boxing was a sport requiring little in the way of expensive equipment, and it was, as one old-timer put it, 'a way you could lift yourself above the rest'. Skating at the Glaciarium continued to be popular, and, until it closed in the fifties, 'nearly everyone you knew was down at the Glacie.'

Some weren't. For the committed and also for those in search of free entertainment, the churches continued to offer the hardy perennials of socials, clubs and meetings. Mavis Kenny, who used to join in the taunts of 'Catholics, Catholics ring the bell/While the Protestants go to hell' when socially appropriate, did not hesitate to sample what was on offer from the enemy:

> I used to go to the old time silent pictures they put on at St Barnabas—you always had to sing the hymns and say the prayers and then on came the pictures. And there was old Fluka . . . I will make you fishers of men . . . He was a nice old fella with glasses . . . played a concertina.

---

19 Anon, *Over a Century of Brewing Tradition—The Story of Tooth & Co.*, (1955), pp 44, 59.
20 Ibid, p 43.

This last was a reference to missionary James Fluker of the City Mission, who specialised in open air preaching. In 1936 he was taken to court for obstructing the traffic, which suggests that he was successful at drawing an audience.[21]

Other street activities continued much as they had for years, with cricket games, fist fights, and crowds of men spilling out of the many pub doors and onto the footpaths when six o'clock closing came round. Dining out might be at a Cahills Restaurant, which had its warehouse in Chippendale and outlets all over the city, or at a Repins Coffee Shop, or, at the bottom end of the market, 'The Hole in the Wall' at Central Railway, opposite Christ Church, where the staple fare was 'pie and peas'.

Recreation was often strongly linked to the workplace. Tooths held balls in its own ballroom on the top floor of the brewery, published an in-house journal (*K.B. Chronicle*), entered lavish floats in street parades, and had its own football team, as well as other sporting clubs.[22] The Christmas Party, held in work hours, was free, but also compulsory, and failure to attend resulted in docked pay. All these practices were intended to create loyalty to the firm and an atmosphere of shared interest between employers and workers. Lois McEvoy recalled that in 1947 when she married John McEvoy, of the family who owned Fostars Shoe factory, the reception was held in the factory canteen, and on arrival the wedding party was greeted by factory workers who had come to wish the couple well. These people were mostly women and presumably mostly local, because it was a Saturday afternoon. This firm and many others also held social functions and ran organised sports clubs. Not all Chippendale workers experienced this kind of employer-employee relationship, however. Many worked at the railways, where social clubs were both directed and patronised by the workers. And the Chippendale men who worked on the docks would no more have socialised with the bosses than they would have voted for Mr Menzies. By the end of the 1950s these social activities were on the wane and Chippendale itself was in rapid decline.

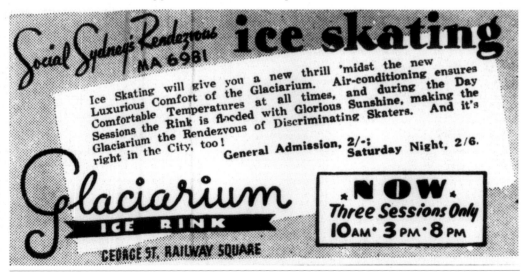

Social Sydney's Rendezvous **ice skating**

MA 6981

Ice Skating will give you a new thrill 'midst the new Luxurious Comfort of the Glaciarium. Air-conditioning ensures Comfortable Temperatures at all times, and during the Day Sessions the Rink is flooded with Glorious Sunshine, making the Glaciarium the Rendezvous of Discriminating Skaters. And it's right in the City, too! General Admission, 2/-; Saturday Night, 2/6.

Glaciarium ICE RINK

★ **NOW** ★ *Three Sessions Only* 10 AM · 3 PM · 8 PM

GEORGE ST, RAILWAY SQUARE

21 June Owen, *The Heart of the City*, p 101.
22 Personal communications, Ted O'Connell, Tooth & Co Ltd, North Sydney, 1989.

Top: The Fostars Sports Club 1940–41. Vic Garry, centre front, was coach. The men played cricket, the women played 'cricko'. *Bottom:* The Brewery Band.

Concentration of industry was at the railway end of the district, between Regent and Abercrombie streets. According to the map there were about 130 houses, plus the Strickland flats, while the streets from Abercrombie to City Road contained about 340. The most residential streets, such as Shepherd, Rose and Myrtle, contained many terrace houses of late nineteenth century vintage, most of them run down. There was little movement out of them in the 1950s as building materials were short and any house was in high demand, but with the easing of wartime restrictions and the new prosperity, the 1960s saws an exodus of just about anyone who could afford the mortgage repayments on a suburban freestanding house. What the planners had failed to do in the 1920s and 1930s, it appeared the residents would do themselves now that new-found wealth gave them the option. That, according to the 'oldtimers', was the end of Chippendale. In the sixties 'everyone just left'.

'Everyone', however, did not leave, although the population was reduced by a hefty 18.6 per cent between 1961 and 1971, as Table 2 indicates.

Table 2: CHIPPENDALE; POPULATION and RESIDENTIAL DENSITY, 1954–1986

	Male	Female	Total	Occupied Dwellings	Persons/ Hectare*
1954	1561	1239	2800	755	40.3
1961	1430	1028	2458	N/A	35.4
1966	1200	1006	2206	633	31.8
1971	1114	887	2001	677	28.8
1976	835	664	1499	573	21.6
1981	824	578	1402	492	20.2
1986	899	638	1537	623	22.1

*This area includes Central Station goods yards and Prince Alfred Park. Density of persons per hectare for the most residential section of Chippendale, west of Balfour Street to City Road, was 93.13 in 1954 and 54.8 in 1986.

Source: Calculated from unpublished census district figures, ABS, Census 1954–86.

However, to long-standing residents, it seemed as though more people were leaving than this table indicates, because the old familiar faces were going as the ethnic composition of the population changed. The conversion of St Paul's Anglican Church into the headquarters of the Greek Orthodox Church in Sydney symbolised these changes, which are represented in Table 3. Although this table shows a stable and high percentage of Australian-born residents, many more of these in 1986 would have been the children and children's children of non-British immigrants, so that the ethnicity in cultural terms was more mixed than the table indicates. Furthermore, commonsense and oral history suggest that the traditional long-term residents who moved away were more often the younger ones, so that the sharp reduction in numbers of children, which the census records, was forcefully experienced by an ageing traditional population who 'knew' that the streets were becoming devoid of children playing or families streaming down Abercrombie Street on Sundays for morning mass.

In the 1950s, Italians, Greeks and British migrants came to Chippendale. Many bought houses instead of renting them, and maintained their fabric, which might otherwise have rotted away. But the southern Europeans did not stay long, soon moving on and out, and the largest increases in recent years have been of non-Europeans. The substantial 13.5 per cent of 'other' residents contained no large groups from particular nations, but an array of different origins. There were some Vietnamese and Lebanese, which were significant migrant groups nationally, but in Chippendale many were from a wide variety of Asian, African and South American countries, suggesting that the area was becoming attractive to students and academics, as the University of Sydney across City Road went through a rapid expansion. Students had lived in Chippendale for many decades, especially in boarding houses in the City Road vicinity, where former wealthy residences were maintained by putting them to this commercial use. But with changing customs and growing affluence, more students now sought rental accommodation in houses and flats, which provided greater autonomy than boarding houses could give. The University itself began to spread over the residential areas around it, eventually taking almost the whole of Darlington and parts of Redfern for engineering faculty and other buildings, but expansion stopped at the boundaries of Chippendale.

In addition to the new value placed on inner residential housing by migrants and students, almost as soon as the traditional residents deserted these areas, urban theorists began to argue in their favour. First came the reinstatement of such suburbs as Paddington and Balmain as desirable middle class addresses, and then the less residentially pure inner areas, like Surry Hills and Darlinghurst. By the seventies all the arguments of earlier decades were being turned on their heads, with the champions of inner city living

Table 3: BIRTHPLACE
1961–86

	1961 %	1976 %	1986 %
Australia	69.8	72.3	68.1
New Zealand	0.8	1.9	4.1
UK and Ireland	6.2	6.5	8.5
Greece/Italy	9.9	3.2	1.8
Other European Countries	9.9	8.4	4.0
Other	3.4	7.7	13.5

Source: Calculated from unpublished census district figures, ABS, censuses 1961–86.

deprecating the suburbs as a barren cultural wilderness. Just as at the beginning of the century, Lord Mayor Taylor and his land-resuming cohorts had 'known' that inner city housing must give way to commercial and industrial building, so now urban enthusiasts 'knew' that any further destruction of old housing had to cease, and people had to be encouraged back into the city to live. It cannot be claimed that the streets of Chippendale had caught their imagination to any degree, but once residential land values in preferred areas had risen high enough to be prohibitive for many would-be home buyers, the impact of the 'back to the city movement' was also felt here.

However, a growing fashion for inner city livng will not simply be accommodated without taking into account the requirements of other land users, and town planning ideology does not carry much force when more powerful interests are at stake. Powerful industrial land users do not conveniently bow out, except when it is in their market interests, or when political decisions force them to do so. In recent decades many of Chippendale's traditional industries were leaving for rational economic reasons, but new kinds of industries were also moving in, and the dominant land user, the brewery, showed no inclination to relocate. And so the scene was set for a confrontation of opposing interests which rivalled the community protests of 1911.

In 1971 the City Council produced its first Strategic Plan for the city. [23] This had no legal force behind it, but it signalled a new concern for maintaining inner city housing, greening the city's streets and 'urban renewal'. The city was divided into 'precincts', each with an 'action plan' for future development. But while the Strategic Plan waxed lyrical over potential restoration of some city areas, it presented Chippendale as a problem area, which contained 'necessary but unglamorous uses'. The Department of Main Roads planned to run a southern distributor through the middle of it, and the Council foreshadowed the need for 'rearrangement of internal streets and lanes' in what it called 'the Brewery Precinct'. Chippendale, a name which they chose to apply only to the western end of the district near City Road, was acknowledged to have 'a good stock of terrace houses meriting protection'. [24] But by the time the Council's planners had embarked on their action plan for Chippendale in 1974, they were more positive about the area. The plan did not advocate the removal of industrial functions, and there was an understanding that the brewery had no plans to relocate, but for the rest 'light industrial activities' only should be allowed, and medium density residential development encouraged.

Partly this turnaround was brought about by a growing understanding that with industrial expansion, Chippendale was fast becoming an obsolete industrial location, due to the small size of many of the factory sites. Several firms, including Scanlens Sweets, Bennett and Barkell, and Fostars Shoes, which closed down in 1958, were occupying more than one site as early as the 1950s. As well as needing more operating space, by the 1960s there was pressure on employers to provide parking space for employees, since increasing numbers were driving cars. In the narrow congested streets of Chippendale this caused

---

23 Council of the City of Sydney, *City of Sydney Strategic Plan*, SRC, 1971, pp 88, 91.
24 Ibid.

Old Building, new industry, corner Abercrombie and Teggs Lane, 1989.

chaos, and encouraged a further buying up of houses. By the early 1970s a row of houses in Goold Street had been flattened for car spaces, and various other sites went the same way. Some of these were previously industrial sites, made available as industries began to move out into industrial parks and outer suburbs, allowing for the expansion of those which stayed behind. Warehousing replaced manufacturing in some cases. In addition to land pressure there was the problem of the ever-increasing size of commercial vehicles, which did not fit well into narrow lanes. Joanne Jennings, recalling her days of working at the White Wings cake factory in Meagher Street before it was removed to Kingsgrove in the early 1980s, said she used to watch fascinated while the trucks manoeuvred their way into and out of 'the skinniest street I've ever seen'.

A Council survey in 1974 showed that ten large firms accounted for three quarters of the area's employees, but that there was also an increase in small firms engaged in light industry and wholesaling, especially in the printing/publishing area.[25] By the eighties many of these had metamorphosed into related activities. The Anglican Press in Queen Street became the site of Data Card (Aust) Limited, an early example of the transition between related industries which would result in a concentration of small firms of wholesalers to the computer industry. Such firms had no need for vast space or cumbersome trucks, but aside from that the reasons for choosing a Chippendale location seemed to be ones of

25 Council of the City of Sydney, *Chippendale Apprendices. 1976 (to Chippendale Action Plan)*, SCR, pp 67–68.

A new face for the old White Wings factory, Meagher Street.

historical linkage. These kinds of firms not only produce no traditional industrial wastes, grime or noise, but some of them, for marketing reasons, have shown an interest in refurbishing their buildings so as to put on a pleasant face to the outside world.

As factories became vacant, other interests moved in. By the late 1970s at least three were used by up to sixty artists as studio space, and some little galleries had appeared. A few good restaurants followed. The Council's Recreation Centre, kindergarten and playground in Pine Street provided a focus for community groups. In 1978, the plan to carve the southern distributor through the area was shelved by the Wran Labor government, and while this ensured continued high levels of through traffic, it also maintained housing. Other industrial sites, like Scanlens Sweets factory and Motor Funerals on City Road, were being bought out by developers interested in building apartments and flats which they anticipated would attract university workers, while other factories were being refitted to serve as apartments. The first recycling of a four-storey factory in Blackfriars Street, restyled as the City Mews, sold out quickly and several similar projects followed in the early eighties. Prices began to rise for Chippendale property, as middle class buyers moved in, inspiring the tag of 'the new Balmain—without the water'. [26]

26 Graham Williams, 'Chippendale: the Old Ghetto Becomes a Poor Man's Balmain', *SMH*, 28 March 1981, p 44.

Table 4: CHIPPENDALE'S TEN LARGEST EMPLOYERS, 1974

Tooths Brewery	1000+
Scanlens Sweets and White Wings	100-150
Eagle & Globe Steel Co Ltd	100
Berlei Hestia	550
Sunny Textiles	200
Land Newspaper)	
Litho-Scans Pty Ltd)	
Publicity Press Ltd)	50-250
Sungravure Pty Ltd)	

Source: Chippendale Appendices (See note 26).

Old terraces, being restored.

Table 5: INDICATORS OF CHIPPENDALE'S CHANGING OCCUPATIONS

Down	1961 %	1986 %
Manufacturing	33.5	8.8
Building and construction	6.8	2.3
Transport/storage	8.8	3.6
Up		
Finance/Property	0.7	12.5
Community Services	4.8	16.7
Public Authorities	1.7	7.9
Home Duties	16.2	19.0

Wholesaling/retailing remained stable. The 1986 figures suggest a more varied mix of occupations. These figures measure the occupations of people living in the area, not necessarily working in the area.

Source: calculated from unpublished census district figures, ABS, censuses 1961, 1986

Tensions developed between the various alternative user groups: students and community groups wanted the area to remain low cost, and pressed for housing co-operative schemes for urban poor and Aborigines. The artists, film developers and other groups hoping for a Sydney Soho were similarly concerned. Claims of rent hikes and evictions followed. The changing composition is clearly indicated in the census figures, which show a marked shift away from manufacturing employment.

But the area did not instantly boom, and many industries remain. Most notably the brewery not only remained, but continued its dogged expansion into residential land. It had been buying up houses opposite the Irving Street brewery, and in O'Connor and Abercrombie streets, in order to demolish them to install forty-nine new fermentation tanks. In March 1977, ignoring petitions from Chippendale residents against this, the Council approved the company's application which included installation of a service bridge 'of light and attractive design' over Carlton Street. [27] From the residents' point of view this meant expansion, reduced right of way and another declaration of the brewery's intention to stay put in Chippendale. From the Council's point of view it meant that they would no longer have to maintain streets which were used almost exclusively by the brewery, and they would be compensated for it as well. In August 1980 they agreed to ask Tooths for $162,780. By then the tanks were being installed and the streets were full of

27 RC 14 March 1977.

construction equipment. Temporary closures were followed by final payment and gazettal of permanent closure in 1982. [28]

Tooths had long held a reputation for being a good landlord, charging small rents and maintaining the properties in good order, a policy which minimised any disquiet at the time of purchase, but when the time came, expansion meant that houses had to go. In the past this had been achieved without many problems, with the brewery taking care to find alternative accommodation or to provide financial inducement. This time was no exception, in that the company allowed tenants rent-free accommodation for up to twelve months, helped find alternative housing and paid their removal expenses. [29] With a few exceptions, people went quietly, but this did not stop a more widespread community reaction against the industrial expansion. Meetings were held and newspaper articles written, some by Robert Tickner, alderman and residents' advocate on Council. The protest was not only about loss of houses, but about the Council's apparent failure to adhere to its own plans for the area, and about concerns for the polluting effects of 'a hazardous and offensive industry'. [30] One resident's account tells it in terms of a struggle for the interests of small people against powerful private and public organisations:

When the brewery started pulling down places, people went to the local member . . . and they had the big meeting down at the Town Hall. Well I went although I don't live in a brewery house. We went up into the high gallery where you can look down. Leo Port was the Mayor then and he had all the paraphernalia on. He said at the time they were looking to be elected, he put out his Action Plan to make Chippendale more residential. Well he gave permission to the brewery to pull three streets down, all

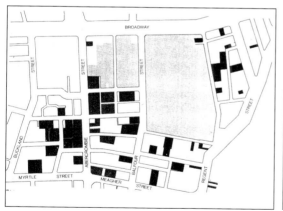 

The maps indicate to what extent between 1949 and 1979 residential premises (dark areas) diminished and the Brewery holdings (shaded grey areas) increased.

28 RC 27 September 1979; 11 September 1979; 11 September 1980; 20 October 1980; NSCR/CRS 116/39 08 0013.
29 NSCA CRS 34//3060/76, Petition regarding Abercrombie development DA 619/76.
(held at Surry Hills Branch, City Library).
30 E.g. Robert Tickner, 'Where Have All the People Gone?', letter to editor, *Peoples Paper,* Vol.2, No.2, March 1977
(held at Surry Hills Branch, City Library).

Irving Street, all along where the shops were and up in O'Connor Street, to build . . . well you know, you've seen it down there . . . Well do you know, they reckoned that was only semi-industrial. Anyhow, the Labor women say, 'What about the Action Plan?' Well it's their plan and they should own it and none of them would. So I sang out, 'What about the Action Plan?' The next minute two ushers were going to throw me out the back door (laughter) . . . They don't worry about the man in the street. They worry about what they can get from the developers.

A Wellington Street resident, Margaret Watts, recorded her experience in her notebook, in 1988:

When we first came to live in Wellington Street the part of the brewery opposite our house was used for unloading the kegs made of steel. The trucks used the entry in Balfour Street. Unloading started at 6 am and often went on till 11 pm. Since the brewing section has been relocated this has all ceased. Fall out from brewery casts a sticky mist over everything. It felt like fine rain out of a cloudless sky.

About five or six years ago the brewery demolished most of the buildings in the block bounded by Broadway, Kensington, Wellington and Balfour streets. They started this one day when I was out and when I came home I thought there must have been a hurricane or something because the whole of the interior of my house was covered with black dust. This went on for months till all the demolition was finished. The final part was like something out of a science fiction movie to watch, or maybe it looked prehistoric. The work began early in the morning under powerful lights. Behind a wall about fifteen feet high was a long building of which I could see the roof from my

Left: Demolition in O'Connor Street, 1989. *Right*: Apartments in Blackfriars Street.

Old style, new tastes, corner Meagher and Regent streets, 1989.

bedroom balcony. The workmen were using one of those enormous machines which take bites out of buildings to smash them up. I couldn't see the mechanical part on the ground, it was hidden by the wall, just the neck and jaws of the thing as it slowly chewed on the roof and walls, occasionally putting its head under a piece to push it off. It looked for all the world like a dinosaur at its meal. I think the part of the brewery which fell to it would have been the older part.[31]

The Brewery had permission to rebuild on this site, provided that demolitions and construction occurred only between 7.30 am and 5 pm and provided that all work complied with noise and emission control regulations. The Brewery had also to contribute to the Council's Public Housing Trust Fund, an amount equal to two per cent of the estimated cost of the development. This two per cent levy, which the Council intended to apply to all large commercial\industrial developments, was later ruled invalid by the courts.[32]

The houses came down, the fermentation vats went in and the roads were closed. 'Light bridges' across the roads turned into visually unattractive pipes and gangways. The consolidation of the brewery on this site was furthered in the 1980s by the clearing of most of the old plant in the original site between Kensington and Balfour streets and the erection of new buildings.[32] It was probably always fairly clear that the brewery would stay.

---

31 RC 21 June 82.

32 Ibid.

Modern change was most obvious to long term residents, who could remember a different Chippendale in their own lives. Late in the 1980s, Mavis Kenny, who was then living in a little old 1840s terrace house in Kensington Street, recalled New Year's Eve celebrations before World War II, as if they were recent events:

'Around twelve o'clock we'd get out the front in the middle of Abercrombie Street—and all the streets around—and you'd hold hands and the boats whistled and cars goin' by honked. It was real rowdy. Now, you could shoot a gun up the street and you wouldn't hit anybody.

There'd be great big bonfires going. I won't mention his surname, but Les—he lived in Abercrombie Street and his backway ran into that little street at the side. Well, he lit two fires, one in there and one in Abercrombie Street. Well, the police came, because it would get that bad for the electric wires. They'd finish up bringing out the fire brigade. Well, while the police were saying "no more on this fire", Les would be out the back, feeding the other one, and when they ran round there when that one was getting too high, he'd run out the front and put more on the other one.

One chap . . . he'd get blind drunk and you had to watch him because all your fences would go. "I'll tear down Abercrombie Street" he used to say. Most of the neighbours used to save up stuff for the fires for a month or two before . . . half the people that were dancing around them would be as full as a tick any'ow . . . The fires were all over Sydney. In the war, because of the blackouts, they weren't allowed, but they still had them.'

In August 1980, in response to public objections and pressure from aldermen, the Council agreed to defer the sale of the streets until a public meeting had been held, but when this produced a swift response from Tooths requesting reassurance that the decision to sell would not be refused, the Council quickly reaffirmed this by resolution.[33] The growth of resident action groups in the seventies, and attempts of people like the Council's planners to encourage ordinary people to have their say, can and did change climates of opinion, but could not match this powerful private interest.

In 1982 some fifty residents responded to a Council survey about their area.[34] Respondents perceived the problems to be many, ranging from dirt, vermin and brewery odours to inadequate shops, parks and trees. In describing it they recorded many different Chippendales:

– *it is a very pleasant and stimulating area;*
– *black soot is everywhere—how plants survive is a wonder;*
– *this unique little suburb;*
– *I hope to learn to like it.*

---

33 RC 11 August 1980; 1 September 1980.
34 CCS Environmental Planning Records 1973–83, A85/138 box 3.

In 1990 Chippendale was in a state of transition. Signs of residential renewal were visible, but so were examples of the degradation of amenities. St Benedict's School closed its doors to students at the end of 1981 and the sale of the Blackfriars School to private interests was imminent, with residents fearful that its actual physical survival may be at risk. The brewery has changed ownership and name, but remains secure on its site. In the space of a few hundred metres it is possible to enjoy a fashionable cut lunch in pleasant gardens which flourish on soil that Thomas Shepherd long ago knew to be excellent for growing plants, or to wander down lanes lined with derelict industrial buildings. The housing ranged from a few of Robert Cooper's Elim Place cottages to fancy new townhouses, and the population is varied in origins and occupations. In the division of the local government area of the city in 1988 most of Chippendale was allocated to the South Sydney City Council, thus severing the connection with the city which went back to 1842, and cutting the area in two administratively. It is too early to assess the impact of this change. However, a few decades ago the future of the place looked bleak. Today, the possibilities seem more varied.

Old factory, modern apartment, Blackfriars Street.

Postscript, 2008

The first edition of this book ended on a cautious note. There was some recognition of improved local conditions. The trend towards creating a more residential Chippendale was in evidence in small factory-to-housing conversions, while street plantings and upgrading of local eateries and pubs accompanied a tentative revitalisation of the area.

On the other hand, Chippendale was still home to many from necessity, rather than choice. Loss of population had resulted in school closures, with the imminent sale of Blackfriars School and its possible demolition singled out as an indication of the threatened heritage of this unloved area of the city. Above all, the enduring interests of long standing and ever expanding industrial giant, the brewery, made it difficult to predict Chippendale's future. According to the text, it was 'fairly clear that the brewery would stay'.

That was then, as they say. Alternatively, let it stand as a cautionary tale for any historians attempting future prediction.

The brewery, which had increasingly dominated the landscape of Chippendale since it was first established by Newnham and Tooth in 1835, was bought out by brewing giant, Carlton and United, in 1983. Right up until the time of sale, Tooths had been physically expanding the operations, and the plant that Carlton took over had just been subjected to several years of extensive modernisation and rebuilding.[1] Carlton continued to upgrade until at least 1991, installing new filtration plant, boiler house, and carbonation facilities. At that time it was the second largest brewery in Australia, and the most automated of the Carlton and United plants.[2]

But in the mid-1990s there was talk of the brewery closing, and while negotiations between workers and management resulted in a temporary stay of execution, operations were being gradually wound back.[3] The firm continued to acquire land up until 1998, but more for the value it might add to the site than for expansion of the plant.

South Sydney City Council administered Chippendale from 1998 until 2003 when it was returned to its traditional home within the boundaries of the City of Sydney. In 1996 South Sydney raised the goal posts for future development by listing Chippendale as a 'conservation area'. Conservation of industrial heritage was, and continues to be, difficult ground to traverse.

Finally, early in 2003 the six hundred workers learned that the brewery would close. A Conservation Management Plan that had been undertaken in 1991 on the assumption that the brewery would remain operational was by-passed in the following years as assets had

---

1 ANU Archives of Business and Labour Z223/121 Tooth and Company, Kent Brewery Redevelopment, cited in Noel Bell Ridley Smith and Partners, *Former Carlton and United Brewery Site, Conservation Plan of Management*, May 2005 (7 volumes), Vol 2, pp 88–92.

2 Ibid, pp 92, 93.

3 Jim Marr, *Last Drinks*, Workers Online, <http://workers.labour.net.au/features/200305/b_tradeunion_carlton.html

been gradually removed and remaining machinery deteriorated.[4] The last beer was brewed there in January 2005.

Questions concerning which of the brewery's buildings would be retained, along with decisions of how much and what kinds of other development would be permitted on the site would exercise many minds and generate many more reports after 2003. With six hectares of precious central Sydney land up for grabs, the debates were intense. In addition, the demise of the brewery, along with its associated noise and odours, would have knock-on effects for the value of all other Chippendale property.

In 2003 the prospective purchaser, Australand, Carlton and United, and the City Council ran a joint architectural design competition to inform the preparation of planning controls for the site. None of the proposals entirely satisfied the judging panel, with the majority opinion being that the results were providing for too much density and height. It was decided to request that the owner hold off submitting an application to develop the site until a new Local Environment Plan was prepared, with revised controls. At this stage the site was placed under a conditional sale to Australand, and Carlton commissioned a second, hugely detailed Conservation Management Plan 'to guide the site owners in the management of cultural heritage resources during the decommissioning and disposal of the brewery and its assets'.[5] Faced with a collection of more or less inoperable machinery, with parts missing and support systems 'degraded', this new study of the significance of the plant struggled to come up with proposals that would maintain any meaningful understanding of the site, given that huge industrial buildings needed to be emptied of equipment if other uses were to be found for them.[6]

This multi-volume study was issued in May 2005. There now existed a detailed history of just about every inch of the site, above and below ground level, extensive interviews with former workers, and endless plans and inventory sheets covering every conceivable detail of the place. The only thing missing was the purchaser, as altered economic circumstances and complex planning issues resulted in the conditional agreement of sale to Australand being rescinded in March 2005.

Various planning controls for the site were developed and exhibited, refined and fought over by planning authorities and interested parties. How high? How dense? How much sunlight? How 'sustainable'? How much of the old fabric to keep? Plans included a park, child care facilities, a community centre, a heritage-friendly Brewery Square.

In mid-2006 the Minister for Planning, Frank Sartor, alleging that progress was too slow and convoluted, used powers under the planning legislation to declare the site to be of 'state significance', thereby making himself the consent authority. He set up his own 'expert advisory panel' and received yet another report from the land holder.[7] An

---

4 Carlton and United Breweries, with Planning Workshop, Kent Brewery Conservation Plan, July 1991.

5 Noel Bell Ridley Smith and Partners op. cit., Former Carlton and United Brewery Site, Conservation May 2005 (7 volumes).

6 Godden Mackay Logan, 'Kent Brewery Machinery Update', report prepared for ICS Pty Ltd, October 2004.

7 JBA Urban Planning Consultants Pty Ltd, 'Study in Support of State Significant Site and Concept Plan Environmental Assessment Report, Carlton and United Breweries Site, SEPP (Major Projects) 2005 Amendments and Concept Plan'. Submitted to Minister for Planning on behalf of Carlton and United Breweries (NSW) Pty Ltd, October 2006, 3 Vols.

'affordable housing levy' being negotiated at the time was increased in exchange for development concessions, to angry protests from the City. Frozen out of the process, the City Council responded to the Brewery's 'concept plan' with a submission to the Minister maintaining that the density and height of the proposed development are excessive, 'and will result in a poor urban form . . . a stadium like enclosure around the public park'.[8] In early 2007 the Minister approved redevelopment of the site for at least 1,500 apartments, about 2,800 residents, 2,300 car spaces and retail space for 4,800 workers.[9]

In a postscript such as this it would be good to be able to complete the story of the brewery site, but that is not to be. The art deco gateway to Tooths Brewery, with the trade mark rampant white horse, remains a landmark on Broadway, with the words 'Tooth & Co Limited Kent Brewery' still faintly visible beneath the more recent Carlton sign. Built in 1939 after the widening of George Street West, it stands as entrance to a site still waiting its next incarnation.

The story is not much clearer on the southern borders of Chippendale, where the state took over much of the planning through the establishment of the Redfern Waterloo Authority in 2004. Touted as an area to provide for commercial tenancies from a city overflow, as part of a crucial city-airport corridor, and as a place of industrial wind-down and residential build-up, currently there is more being discussed than done, and the outcomes are uncertain. Some of this discussion, predicting negative consequences for the long term Indigenous residents of the area, comes from the Gadigal Information Centre or over the airwaves of Koori Radio, broadcasting 'live and deadly' from Chippendale.

While all around is in flux, the population of Chippendale has been quietly reinventing itself, with a very different profile from the Chippendale of two decades ago. Between the national census of 1996 and the following one in 2001, the residential population of Chippendale increased from 2,015 to 3,241. While residential figures are not the same as those for people who work in the area, the decline of industrial and manufacturing sites, long in evidence, has accelerated since this book was first written. In 2001 the people who lived in Chippendale were young, with 56% aged between 18 and 34 years, compared with 27% for the whole of Sydney. There was a high representation of professionals, with this youthful population earning weekly household incomes that were similar to the metropolitan average. This level of income is all the more significant when the large student population who live in the area is taken into account. Aside from English, the most frequently spoken languages are Chinese, Korean and Vietnamese, and nearly 7% of residents said they were Buddhists, almost twice the Sydney average. The place in Meagher Street once known as the White Wings factory is currently home to the Ching Chung Taoist Association.

While many of Chippendale's residents consider their sojourn here as only temporary, as a group they are part of a profound change to the landscape. Students attending the University of Sydney had always found cheap accommodation in its surrounding

---

8 'City of Sydney submission for concept plan—CUB site', CRS 2006/83042.

9 Robert Harley, 'CUB site clash begins' *Australian Financial Review*, 10 April 2007.

precincts, including Chippendale, and this population has grown rapidly. The Blackfriars School closed its doors at the end of 1989, and the next years witnessed talk of residential towers and car parks, but in 1996 the University of Technology, Sydney took up residence in the old heritage-listed buildings for what they call their 'Shopfront', where community-based projects are undertaken with collaborative inputs of skills and resources from the University students and staff. In the same year, part of the old Grace Brothers department store on Broadway had been converted into student flats with advertisements exhorting the public to invest in the area's greatest asset, education.

The most recent tertiary institution to arrive in Chippendale is the University of Notre Dame, which commenced operations in 1989 in Fremantle, Western Australia. On 1 August, 2004, in St Benedict's Church, Sydney's Archbishop, George Pell, and the Prime Minister, John Howard—in possibly the first official visit of an Australian Prime Minister to Chippendale—launched the first of several proposed Sydney campuses of this 'boutique' university. Enrolments commenced in 2006, with the old St Benedict's school and presbytery forming the nucleus of the campus. Back in 1884, when the state was first seriously entering the field of education, Archbishop Moran, in a reference to the Blackfriars School, had been 'pained and grieved' to see 'other schools encroaching on your ground.' Now in the early 21st century the Federal Government was providing funding for this private university, and the tension was internal to the Catholic Church.

Conspicuously absent from the launch of Notre Dame was the head of the Australian Catholic University and the local priest of St Benedict's, Fr. Terence Purcell, who had ministered to the Chippendale faithful for over thirty years. *The Sydney Morning Herald* reported the launch under the heading 'Turf war sours welcome to these holy gates'. Peter Sheehan, the Vice Chancellor of the Australian Catholic University was reported to have claimed there had been no consultation, while Purcell, never the diplomat, claimed 'Cardinal Pell ordered me to let them in . . . but I don't want them here.'[10] The press happily reported several spats between the priest and His Eminence, with the one claiming the rain came in on his parishioners because the diocese refused to mend the church roof, and the other observing that he recalled no approach for funds, and that in any case the rain could not have effected many people, as the parish was almost dead. One of the benefits of the new arrangements according to Pell was that the university would repair the church.[11] Father Purcell retired from his post under protest in early 2005 and by the end of 2006, at age 84 was himself dead, following a lengthy illness. But not before he was awarded an OAM in recognition of his services to restoration of the 1852 church, achieved in part through generous amounts of his own money.

Now as ever, the issues that define Chippendale concern large scale developments as well as small everyday things. Today a visit to Chippendale might be for the purposes of registering a birth or getting married at the Registry Office, recently relocated from the city centre to Regent Street. Or time might be spent enjoying one of the small galleries in the

---

10 Matthew Thompson, 'Turf war sours welcome at these holy gates,' *SMH*, 2 August 2004.

11 Jano Gibson, 'Notre Dame squeezes into crowded inner Sydney university market' (website of UTS journalism students), first in *Newsday*, 10 September 2004.

area. Or a class at the Council's Pine Street Creative Arts Centre, where programs are provided for children and adults in the transformed Golden Fleece Kindergarten which operated in Pine Street since it first began in a disused boot factory in 1907 until it closed its doors in 2001. Or enjoying a good pub meal before taking in a show at the Seymour Centre, across the road from Chippendale on the corner of City Road and Cleveland Street.

Or setting out to change the world at the Resistance Centre in Abercrombie Street, or visiting 'the sustainable' house in Myrtle Street where private citizen Michael Mobbs has turned an 1890s terrace house into a residence that is off the grid, using solar energy and an internal water treatment system, all operating in a manner that does not detract from expected twenty-first century creature comforts.

Beneath Chippendale there remains the fertile soil and the water flows, now captured in nineteenth century drains, that made it a gathering place for the Gadigal people, and in colonial times contributed to the success of Shepherd's Nursery. But Shepherd grew exotic plants and vines, and subsequent developments covered it all in concrete and tar. Today Chippendale's streets are again filling with eucalypts and angophoras. The development pressures on this piece of urban land are enormous, but familiarity with its history and understanding of its natural underpinnings tell us that there is potential for a richly varied landscape to emerge.

BIBLIOGRAPHY

Anon., *Over a Century of Brewing Tradition: The Story of Tooth and Co.*, Sydney 1955

Margaret Bevage et al., *Worth her Salt*, Hale and Iremonger, Sydney 1982

Robert Burford, *Description of a View of the Town of Sydney*, J. and C. Adlard, London 1829

F.B. Boyce, *A Campaign for the Abolition of the Slums in Sydney*, William Anderson, Sydney, 1913

F.B. Boyce, *Fourscore Years and Seven*, Angus and Robertson, Sydney 1934

Catalogue of Fifty-four Allotments of Land the Property of the Late Solomon Levey Esq. . . . , J. Tegg and Co., Sydney 1838

Michael Christie, *The Sydney Markets*, 1788-1988, Sydney Market Authority, 1988

Frank Clune, *Saga of Sydney*, Angus and Robertson, Sydney 1961

Shirley Fitzgerald, *Rising Damp*, Oxford University Press, Melbourne 1987

Brian Fletcher, *Landed Enterprise and Penal Society*, Sydney University Press, Sydney 1976

J.J. Fletcher, *Blackfriars Public School*

J. Fletcher and J. Burnswood, *Government Schools in New South Wales since 1888*, N.S.W. Education Department, 1988

Bernard G. Judd, *He that Doeth: The Life of Archdeacon R.B.S. Hammond*, Marshall, Morgan and Scott, Edinburgh 1951

Max Kelly (ed.), *Sydney City of Suburbs*, New South Wales University Press, Sydney 1987

F.A. Larcombe, *The Advancement of Local Government in New South Wales 1906 to the Present*, Sydney University Press, Sydney 1978

F.A. Larcombe, *The Origin of Local Government in New South Wales*, Vol. 1, Sydney University Press, Sydney 1973

G.J.R. Linge, *Industrial Awakening,* Australian National University Press, Canberra 1979

A.G. Lowndes (ed.), *South Pacific Enterprise*, Angus and Robertson, Sydney 1956

Michael Matthews, *Pyrmont and Ultimo: A History*, self published 1982

Stuart McIntyre, *The Oxford History of Australia, Vol. IV 1901–1942*, Oxford University Press, Melbourne 1986

June Owen, *The Heart of the City: The First 125 Years of the Sydney City Mission*, Kangaroo Press, Sydney 1887

Jill Roe (ed.), *Twentieth Century Sydney*, Hale and Iremonger, Sydney 1980

Peter Spearritt, *Sydney since the Twenties*, Hale and Iremonger, Sydney 1978

Tooth and Co. Ltd., *The First Hundred Years: A Brief History of Kent Brewery*, Tooths, Sydney 1935.

Sources of Illustrations

INDEX